What Schools Are For

by

John I. Goodlad

///

University of California, Los Angeles

and

Institute for Development of
Educational Activities, Inc.

A Publication of the Phi Delta Kappa Educational Foundation

Cover design by Victoria Voelker

For Irving

Publication of this monograph has been financed in part through a generous contribution from Miss Bessie Gabbard, a member of the Ohio State University Chapter of Phi Delta Kappa and a member of the Board of Governors of the Phi Delta Kappa Educational Foundation.

Contents

Preface

This monograph was written to be read quickly — ideally in one sitting. It is my preference that the ideas contained in it be reflected upon, not chewed on, in the reader's own effort to answer the questions raised. The questions are more important than my answers to them.

What follows was stimulated in large part by two troubling aspects of schooling today in the United States of America. First, we are impatient — more than at any other time in my memory — with talk about fundamental issues pertaining to what kinds of individuals schools should seek to develop, what kinds of experiences young people should have in schools, and most of all, what education is. The discussion that should be taking place in homes, on television, in state capitols, and especially among educators, simply is not going on. Second, and closely related, we have filled up the void with ill-conceived action. The old slogan prevails: Don't just stand there, do something!

Unfortunately, much of what we have done and continue to do has resulted in trivialization of the ends and means of schooling. Recent research suggests that schools spend an inordinate amount of time on noninstructional activities. Regrettably, much of the time spent on instruction is devoted to training. As a consequence, today's schools are only marginally educational institutions.

The answer to improving our schools can be stated simply: Make them be primarily educational in all that they do. But stating and effecting what is required are two different things, the latter being made especially difficult because we seem not to know or have forgotten what education is. My conception of education runs counter to much of what is done in and proposed for schools.

I write in praise of the common school — the concept, not what most states and many local school boards currently are mandating that our schools become. Never before has the common school been in such danger — ironically, from those who claim to be its friends, as well as from those traditional enemies who never much believed in education for the masses anyway. While its presumed friends squabble over who will control school policies and practices, other persons lay plans for alternatives that are not likely to take care of the unfinished business of the common school. I am all for alternatives to the traditional system of schooling, but if these are to be more viable educationally than what we presently have, they must be available to all. The concept of the common school stands.

If my writing becomes strident at times, it is because I feel the urgency created by our "frivolous inertia," to use Whitehead's words, when it comes to talking and thinking about our most critical educational issues. In reviewing one of my books (*Facing the Future*, 1976), Cynthia Parsons, education editor of the *Christian Science Monitor*, was kind enough to write the following: ". . . [T]his gentle scholar, long associated with calling for the best in schooling, is welcome at every educator's meeting, and his books, monographs, and shorter writings are in every teacher's room and in every teacher training institution. But few seem to hear his primary thesis. . . ." Perhaps I have been too gentle, too soothing.

Much of what I say in this monograph is not gentle. And I spare no group — legislators, chief state school officers, superintendents, principals, teachers, teacher educators, researchers, or lay citizens — for either the present unsatisfactory condition of our schools or for what must be done to reconstruct them. Some of my friends may hear me saying things differently from what they think they have heard me say before and will be disappointed. Some of those persons who have disagreed with me in the past will be pleased at times — but only at times.

I have written before about what schools are for. Several recent papers were written with the preparation of this book in mind, and I have drawn from them: "On the Cultivation and Corruption of Education," *The Educational Forum*, 42 (March 1978), 267-78; "Accountability: An Alternative Perspective," The 1978 De Garmo Lecture, Society of Professors of Education; "The Trouble with Humanistic Education," *Journal of Humanistic Education* (January/February 1978), 8-29; "Educational Leadership: Toward the Third Era," *Educational Leadership*, 35 (January 1978), 322-24, 326-27, 329-31; and "What Schools Are For: A Transatlantic Dialogue," The Sir John Adams Lecture,

University of London Institute of Education, October 1977. The first section of Chapter Four was published as an article, "Can Our Schools Get Better?" *Phi Delta Kappan*, 60 (January 1979), 342-47.

I had hoped to write free of the notes, footnotes, and references associated with academic writing. The invitation from the Phi Delta Kappa Educational Foundation asked me to write a little book on what was uppermost in my mind. (The invitation's suggestion about setting aside a few weeks in the summer to do the job implied less than I wanted to hear about the state of my mind and more than I believed possible for my pen; it also proved overly optimistic on both counts). For one thing, I discovered that I needed to read; reading always impedes writing. I read new things and old things, discovering along the way some choice passages that said more than was on my mind. And so there are references — a modest number. However, they are used almost exclusively for documentation and are listed for each chapter at the end of the volume rather than at the end of each chapter. Consequently, there is no need to break off from the narrative in order to pursue footnotes.

This book would not have been written had there not been the aforementioned invitation. About this I have mixed feelings. It took far more time than I had anticipated; almost everything does. Nonetheless, the request forced me to think and write more clearly on some themes that are often on my mind. For this I am grateful to the Phi Delta Kappa Educational Foundation.

This has been a rather lonely undertaking. I should be able to thank various friends and professional colleagues for reading and offering suggestions to improve the manuscript. But I did not ask anyone to do so. I suppose I feared that, if I did, the book would never see the light of day. Patricia A. Bauch, Lillian K. Drag, and Anna J. Edwards assisted in various aspects of the manuscript's preparation and for their good work I am most appreciative.

John I. Goodlad
March 1979

Chapter One

Perspectives and Definitions

On the last day of March 1968, I embarked on a short trip that will always remain fresh in my memory. On the overnight flight from Los Angeles to London, the captain apologized for waking the passengers early but said he could hold back the news no longer. President Lyndon B. Johnson had announced that he would stop the bombing in Vietnam and would not run for reelection in the fall.

Four days later, I disembarked from the return flight and went directly to my car in the parking lot. The radio went on with the starting of the engine and the words seemed to fill the small space around me. Martin Luther King had been assassinated.

What have these two incidents to do with the subject of what schools are for? Actually, a great deal. Both men had high expectations for education and schooling. Three years before, laying the groundwork with Congress for the monumental Elementary and Secondary Education Act of 1965, President Johnson had said that, if one looks deeply enough, education is found to be at the heart of all our problems. Addressing the White House Conference on Education a few months later, with the bill now enacted, Vice President Hubert Humphrey proclaimed that we would go down in history as the nation that used its educational system to deal successfully with the problems of poverty, unemployment, slum clearance, and, indeed, world peace. Is this what schools are for?

Part of Martin Luther King's dream was that our institutions, "the bones of our civilization," would play their part in the cause of social and economic justice for all. Integrated schools would assist in eliminating prejudice and assuring equality of educational and career opportunity for people who had long been denied both. Is this what schools are for?

In a graduate seminar I taught from the late 1960s to the mid-1970s, I usually began with the question, "What are schools

1

for?" The student responses invariably paraphrased philosophers from Aristotle to Whitehead and Dewey as they described the acquisition of those presumed virtues of the good person in the good society. Is this what schools are for?

Usually, someone in the group mentioned "baby-sitting." There would be a few laughs, sharply cut off by a mother in the group who would say, in effect, "Don't knock it." Is this what schools are for?

Clearly, schools in our society have performed all of the functions implied above and more. They have served to socialize immigrants; to prepare the young for jobs; to keep young people off the labor market; to foster patriotism; to relieve and free mothers from chores of child rearing and supervision; to develop individual talents; to teach certain facts, concepts, and processes; and on and on. Some who would rewrite American educational history say that they also have served to select winners and losers on the basis of circumstances of birth; to increase the gap between the haves and have-nots in our economic system; to turn off certain kinds of talent while favoring others; and to lower the self-concept of those who do not adjust easily to the expectations and regimens of schooling. What schools have done is not necessarily what they should have done.

Many of the things schools implicitly have been expected to do fail to show up in formal statements of what they are asked to do. For example, baby-sitting does not appear on any list of state goals of schooling. And yet teachers quickly find out how deeply the school's custodial role is embedded in family life when they try to schedule an occasional shortened instructional day for staff development purposes. One would have to examine much more than local and state lists of educational goals to determine the actual functions performed by schools during specific periods in our country's history.

It becomes apparent that there are distinctly different ways of thinking about what schools are for. There are three major sub-questions to the main question: What are schools expected or asked to do? What do schools do? What should schools do? In this monograph I deal with aspects of all three.

Regarding the first, various individuals and groups have different expectations. Some of these are official and take on the character of formal directives, as when legislatures or school boards issue lists of goals or proficiencies. Most are unofficial, resting in the minds of persons interested in schools, and are usually not precisely formed. Nonetheless, these expectations

2

affect what goes on in schools, perhaps more than official pronouncements do. What teachers in Oak Creek Elementary think they should do probably is the most powerful determinant of what the children there actually do each day in the classroom.

Much of what schools are expected to contribute to society does not appear in lists of educational goals. Such has been the case with the aspirations expressed by both Lyndon B. Johnson and Martin Luther King. Yet some of what they sought has been built into the educational system through the specification of guidelines for the expenditure of state and federal funds. Few schools have escaped the programmatic influence of these guidelines.

The goals officially articulated for schools are educational. They imply, with varying degrees of specificity, the kinds of knowledge, skills, and attitudes that students should acquire. But the achievement of these goals occurs within a context of political, social, and economic interests that not only impose additional, more implicit purposes but also determine to a considerable degree the values likely to prevail in school settings. The articulated, official goals may stress cooperation, but competition is more likely to characterize school activity, since competition is the prevailing societal value. College students were acutely aware, during the Sixties, of such discrepancies and inconsistencies.

Determining what various individuals and groups expect from schools is a form of survey research. It is basically sociological, not philosophical. Such inquiry does not tell us what schools do or should do. Given the structure of the American educational system, however, state-approved goals do provide guidelines for evaluating local schools and holding them accountable. Studies comparing parent, student, and teacher expectancies in a given school may help explain tensions between a school and its community. And studies of teachers' stated goals should provide clues to the actual instructional program of a school. They also should reveal the degree of compatibility between teachers' and state-mandated goals. But such studies still leave open to debate the question of what schools *should* seek to do.

A second approach to answering the question of what schools are for is to examine what they do or how they are used. An observer can see: children playing a variety of games at recess, primary classes organized into three reading groups, students and a teacher discussing the structure of Congress, students reading and writing at tables in the school's library. He can see

3

other things, too: junior high students pushing and shoving one another at their lockers in a crowded hallway; two youths, a male and a female, arms around waists, gazing soulfully into each other's eyes; a small child piling blocks and then knocking them down; a fifth-grade boy standing in front of a class, painfully reading from a book and being corrected frequently by the teacher.

One begins to see the difficulties in determining what schools do. It is an overwhelmingly complex task simply to describe the whole picture. Even drawing inferences from a comprehensive description of what schools do is fraught with problems. How similar or different are schools in what they do? When you've seen one high school, have you seen them all?

The level of complexity increases when one attempts to deal with the experiences of those who live and work in schools — students, teachers, administrators, and others. What meaning does school have for them? While a particular school district promulgates a list of 11 major goals emphasizing knowledge, citizenship, personal development, and so on, we would hesitate to conclude that students in that district are acquiring a love of literature and habits of good citizenship. Perhaps they are learning to dislike literature and to cheat and lie. Or, even though the prevailing social policy is for desegregated schools and the official rhetoric stresses integration, segregation prevails inside the schools and racial prejudice is on the rise in the community.

We can make inferences about what a school is being used for by interviewing and observing those who live, work, and play there — but only inferences. The deeper we probe, the more rich and revealing the clues. But any conclusions drawn remain idiosyncratic to the observer. Nonetheless, data of this kind can be useful in suggesting discrepancies between stated goals and what is actually going on. The inferences suggested by such data, much more than the inferences drawn only from articulated goals, get us closer to understanding what schools are used for.

Ironically, the information used most frequently and uncritically to draw inferences and to make judgments about what schools do and how well they do it is derived from measures in very limited areas. Standardized test results apparently carry more weight and are of more interest than data on student dropouts, attitudes toward school, and interest in academic pursuits. Students' good marks tend to lull us into apathy regarding the nature and quality of their programs, their experiences in schools, and the long-term personal impact of those experiences.

Preoccupation with limited, short-term effects probably has retarded interest in the question of what schools do. There has been little disposition on the part of reformers to get data about present programs before recommending new ones. Until very recently, researchers have relied almost exclusively on test scores in judging the adequacy of teaching methods. The prevailing principle is that high achievement scores signal good schools; low scores indicate bad ones. The widespread application of such a principle is simplistic, misleading, and dangerous.

A third approach to the question of what schools are for is to consider what they ideally ought to do. Should they be agents of direct social reform? Should they be used to reconstruct the social order? Should they serve the social order through, for example, providing personnel for the needs of business and industry? Or should schools eschew such instrumental roles and concentrate solely on cultivating the abilities and sensitivities of children and youth? The individuals so educated might well become social reformers, captains of industry, artists, and thoughtful, voting citizens, but they would become these things through cultivation of their unique abilities and personal choice.

The question boils down to whether schools should be used for ends other than or in addition to strictly educational ones. If so, then the next question is whether these ends determine and justify the means. For example, does a long-term shortage of secretaries suggest specific vocational goals for schools with a greater emphasis on business education courses in the secondary school curriculum? Should curricular emphasis shift to computer programming when the need for more programmers shows up in job market analyses? Or is there something more fundamentally educational schools should do that is not so dependent on shifts in employment opportunities? If so, what goals are implied, and are some more desirable than others?

These are classic questions to which some classic responses have been given. I have no aspirations to improve on those answers. But I do take the position that some things are more worthy than others for schools to do — and that these things are best differentiated by one's concept of education. In Chapter Three, I will identify some of these things.

Interestingly, when one asks any group of teachers or laypersons what schools are for, the answer usually takes the form of idealistic "shoulds." Almost always, too, a duality prevails. The *individual* is to learn to read and write, make

5

independent judgments, or develop personal talents, and *society* is to be served through the cultivation of those habits and dispositions thought to lead to responsible citizenship. The list soon becomes repetitive. There usually is general agreement on about a dozen educational goals.

The more specialized and homogenized the group, the more likely that certain economic, social, or political uses will be added to these dozen educational goals. Education and schooling should improve the gross national product, or the welfare of the disadvantaged, or the existing form of government. Politicians find it to their advantage to stress all of these to assure the broadest possible voting appeal.

It is at this philosophical level of speculating about what schools should do that we see forming those forces that influence what schools officially are asked to do. It is the general agreements — the dozen or so goals that become repetitive — that get written into state mandates and expectations. Certainly, these general goals influence what schools actually do, but the special economic, political, and social interests do not appear in these articulated educational goals. Yet they certainly contribute to what schools are used for and they significantly determine the extent to which schools are educational institutions in their daily operation. We see, then, that the question of what schools are for is inextricably tied to the question of what education is.

Definitions

It is not easy, even for discussion purposes, to separate the three approaches to the question of what schools are for. The terms and definitions offered below are not intended to be the last word. They serve, rather, to make certain distinctions essential to what follows.

To repeat, the first approach pertains to what schools are asked, expected, or called upon to do. I refer to these expectations as *goals,* sometimes prefixing the word "educational." The second approach refers to what schools do or are used for. These uses I call *functions,* and I shall deal with two types. The third approach concerns what schools should do. To the extent that schools should be entirely educational, they are to be guided by ideal postulates, which I call *aims.*

The problem in trying to deal neatly and discretely with all three approaches to the question of what schools are for is that schools serve more than educational goals and perform more than educational functions. Further, some of the former are not articulated as expectations and some of the latter are not included in evaluative criteria. Schools are asked to serve social *goals,* some of which are only vaguely or not at all educational. Schools perform social *functions,* some of which are never made explicit and some of which are not educational. Schools never have devoted themselves exclusively to educational *aims* and probably never will. Their goals are derived through a social-political process. The functions they perform reflect certain needs and interests in the surrounding society. Consequently, schools are only in part educational institutions.

Our system of public schooling is called upon again and again to help solve societal problems, as when President Johnson referred to education's role in eliminating unemployment, poverty, and war. It is expected that these problems are to be taken care of, in part, through schooling. Commercial television also is asked to devote a portion of its time to public service programs — in effect, to educate. But the follow-up to such programs usually is assigned to the schools. Education and schooling become one for the achievement of some social purpose.

Rarely, however, do purposes such as the reduction of poverty show up as a specific goal articulated for schools by states and local school districts. The lofty goals stated for schools almost invariably correspond to those ideal statements of "oughts" and "shoulds" that I am calling aims — that is, traits, sensibilities, and understandings to be developed in individuals through education. Noneducational social purposes simply are omitted from lists of goals for schools. Nonetheless, schools fulfill many such social purposes in their day-to-day functioning.

A function, for me, is what something actually performs, does, or is used for. For example, imagine a pump installed for the purpose of pumping water from the sea to a ledge above, from which the water cascades down to a larger pool. This is what the pump did for years; this was its function. But the pump stopped pumping water several years ago. It now serves (functions) as a stopping place for children going to and from school. Whatever its original purpose, the pump now functions as a resting and gathering place.

Such things happen to schools, too. The ultimate test of what schools are for is what they do. What they actually do may bear little relationship to what they are officially asked to do.

An anomaly begins to emerge. At any given time, a society has purposes for its schools, but only some of these are articulated as

7

goals for schooling. Some of them tend to be, according to their wording, educational in character. Consequently, schools perform two sets of functions: 1) social functions not expressly stated as goals and 2) legitimated educational goals (as well as some educational functions not so legitimated). Both sets of functions take up time and resources, the noneducational ones sometimes consuming more than the educational. In appraising the role and performance of schools, however, we concentrate almost exclusively on their educational function — and usually on only a small part of it at that.

Our school system, a huge enterprise, operates as though its social purpose is exclusively educational; it sets goals that are educational, and it is evaluated as though what it does is educational. Meanwhile, it serves purposes appearing to be other than educational, performs functions other than educational, but is generally not evaluated by criteria that are other than educational.

It is possible, I believe, for the functions of schools to be primarily noneducational. Once the balance in what schools do swings predominantly to noneducational functions, what action should a society take? Should it engage in massive reconstruction of its schools or create new institutions?

My own view is that schools are educational institutions. I admit, however, that they always will be called upon to serve other purposes in addition to educational goals. What is imperative is that the educational functions be dominant. Furthermore, education must be evaluated not just according to goal attainment but also according to the means employed. Or, conversely, means must be judged by more than their contribution to predetermined ends.

Criteria for the justification and evaluation of an educational function are found in the aims of education — that is, normative postulates regarding what education is and should do. Criteria for the justification and evaluation of functions that are other than educational must be found elsewhere.

What Follows

In succeeding chapters I will inquire into social purposes of schools and the translation of these purposes into educational goals, the functions of schools, and the aims of education. The thesis advanced is that schools are educational institutions. A question to be examined is whether they function educationally enough of the total time they are in operation to warrant classification as educational institutions. If the answer to this question is yes, then a second question emerges: To what degree is this time utilized in truly educational ways? Or, put differently, Is education in schools advanced or corrupted?

If it appears that schools are only minimally performing educational functions and reform or change appears doubtful, then what are the options? One is to give parents or their children vouchers by which they can secure education in a competitive marketplace. Some existing schools might survive and new ones appear, but the public educational system as we have known it would disappear. A modification of this approach would be to create a partial voucher system. Time spent in school would be sharply reduced; vouchers would be spent for education beyond the "basic" program provided for a few hours each day in schools.

Another alternative would be to legitimate whatever it is that schools now do, but to create new settings to take care of their educational omissions. While this may sound radically innovative, it isn't. The creation of new institutions and agencies to take care of long-neglected or newly perceived needs is characteristic of dynamic societies.

There probably is no single answer to any of these questions. A single answer assumes a common need and diagnosis. The U.S. is a large, complex country, offering extraordinary variety in virtually every aspect of living. It is difficult to believe that schools are fulfilling society's purposes uniformly. It also is difficult to believe that the nation's schools are fulfilling educational goals equally well. Should they be serving the same purposes and goals? Are they? To me it seems sensible to assume that what schools do and should do is not necessarily the same for Manhattan, Kansas, as it is for Manhattan, New York. It also seems sensible to assume that there are some conditions and elements essential to and characteristic of education that are and should be universal.

One of the problems in addressing the questions I have posed is that certain kinds of data simply are not yet available. This has not deterred others from addressing these questions, nor shall I allow this lack to deter me. Of course, most of the questions raised can be answered only partly after we gather quantitative data; for some, such data are of little or no value. In the final analysis, most educational issues are normative in character.

Chapter Two discusses how social purposes have emerged in

9

light of current realities. Some of these purposes are amenable to education and, therefore, are appropriately translated into educational goals. But the distinction as to which are and which are not educational in character is extraordinarily important. Much disillusion with schooling results from asking schools to do what they cannot do well. Unless we change our perspective and accept the notion that schools are only marginally educational institutions, our dissatisfaction with them will increase as they are asked to take on more and more of society's noneducational purposes.

While there is relatively high state-by-state agreement on educational goals articulated for schools, there is much less agreement on the social purposes schools should be asked to achieve. How far schools should go in seeking racial desegregation is a case in point.

Educational goals articulated by the states do not necessarily determine how time is spent in schools. Systems of schooling are not like factories — open at the ends and relatively closed on the sides. Interests other than those officially sanctioned find their way into the system. For example, what parents want or teachers say they are trying to do undoubtedly affects what students in classrooms do. What parents expect and what teachers see as their goals do not tell us precisely what a given school does. But these expectations provide clues that, in turn, provide useful hunches and hypotheses about the ongoing functions of a school.

Various forces in society seek to get their special interests legitimated in educational goals and school programs. What are predominantly economic, political, or social goals take on an educational veneer — sometimes in goal statements, sometimes in pseudo-philosophical rhetoric. The lives of educators, particularly administrators, are complicated by the mixed bag of educational and noneducational expectations coming into all levels of our system of public schooling. Schools serve many masters.

Chapter Three takes us to the question of what education is and what schools should do if they are educational institutions. I break no new ground here. There is a rich literature on the question. And so, for the most part, I borrow from Whitehead and Dewey and more contemporary thinkers such as Norman Cousins, R.S. Peters, Lawrence Cremin, David S. Saxon, and Ralph W. Tyler. This is a diverse group; the diversity is deliberately chosen. There are vast differences among these educational thinkers. But they all have something in common:

They address education, as opposed to training, indoctrination, or some other corruption of it.

One of the major points I seek to make in Chapter Three is that statements of goals simply are not sufficient to guide the conduct of education. We are in and probably will continue to be in a period of infatuation with the endless reduction of goals to a level of specificity designed to assure foolproof step-by-step teaching and learning. This probably is an excellent procedure for learning how to tie one's shoelaces or to smoke salmon, but it probably impedes attainment of those higher literacies that educational institutions are supposed to foster.

The aims of education addressed in Chapter Three include, then, more than a sense of direction. They embrace also some of the conditions and qualities that should characterize the means of educating. As suggested earlier, ends do not justify means. Means have a life of their own and must be judged according to the quality of educational experience they provide.

Chapter Three concludes with a summary and an analysis of the goals for schools that have arisen over the years and are now articulated and legitimated by most of our states. These have arisen out of social purposes and have been adopted for schools because, presumably, they are educational or potentially educational. However, because the needs of society from which these goals were derived initially were not necessarily educational in character, the goals articulated for schools may involve both educational and noneducational activity. The discussion of aims in the first part of Chapter Three is intended to provide some of the guiding criteria to assure that schools emphasize primarily educational activity. Since schools are called upon to do so many things, some of which one would be hard pressed to call educational, it is imperative that potentially educative expectations be maximized. Otherwise, schools soon become only marginally educative.

Chapter Four addresses the corruption of education by society, schools, and school systems. Cultivation of the system of schooling does not necessarily improve the quality of education in schools. And, clearly, intrusion of functions other than education into our schools does not improve education at all; it simply takes time from what is supposed to be the prime function.

Cultivation of the school system for all kinds of social purposes has made schooling one of this nation's largest enterprises. Politicians frequently stake their futures on educational legislation; the organized teaching profession has become one of the largest and most powerful lobbies in state and federal capitols. School boards frequently look for management rather than curricular and instructional experience and capabilities in hiring new superintendents.

Not surprisingly, the improvement of learning figures more prominently in the rhetoric than in the time allocations of school administrators, including principals. Chapter Five is a plea for those in administrative positions to put curricular and instructional matters at the center of their leadership role. Of course, if schools no longer are predominantly educational institutions, then this advice may be misplaced. In which case, perhaps we should rethink the entire structure of what we have created for educating the young.

Although the improvement of educational programs in schools should be at the center of educators' lives, there is always the danger that they will push for what may have dubious educational value. Chapter Five is designed in part to remind school leaders that there are no curricular and instructional panaceas. Good instruction, for example, involves the orchestration of a dozen or more factors. Sound educational leadership provides the support mechanisms teachers need if they are to acquire and use a repertoire of teaching skills.

While Chapter Five addresses improvement of the schools we have, Chapter Six suggests several alternative scenarios for the reconstruction of education and schooling. These range from a vastly reduced role for schools as we know them to a 24-hour day concept of schooling. In the latter, there would be a deliberate effort to encompass and legitimate functions now bootlegged or otherwise imposed on schools without simultaneously providing the resources and structures required for their adequate performance. Differing scenarios might guide schools in different parts of the country. A monolithic system of schooling is neither necessary nor desirable. The appropriate role for schools depends in large part on the educative and potentially educative agencies available in the surrounding community.

It will be noted that no chapter is devoted specifically and exclusively to what schools do. The best answers to the question of what schools do are inferences from various kinds of data: observations of daily practice, interviews with teachers and students, case studies, analysis of teachers' diaries, examination of how federal and state grants are used, studies of the daily activities of specialized personnel, and so on. We do not yet have adequate descriptive data from which to determine similarities and differences in the ways schools conduct their business, let alone the more in-depth material required for drawing inferences about functions and the impact of schools on the individuals in them. Events may be perceived quite differently by different observers.

At the time this book is being written, both ethnographic studies of schools and classrooms and methodological critiques of such studies are attracting the attention of educational researchers. When we have more data on what schools actually do, we will become more conscious of the limitations of achievement test scores as the sole index of school and student functioning. But the data we need for making reasonably adequate inferences about what schools scattered across this vast land do will not come easily. The costs and logistics involved are considerable. The U.S. Office of Education is not yet in a position to fulfill one of its constitutional charges adequately — that is, the provision of periodic reports on the condition of our schools.

Although no single chapter is devoted to an examination of what schools do, my hunches and inferences are scattered throughout this book. They are drawn from a variety of sources: studies with colleagues,[1] studies by others, and both firsthand impressions from visiting schools and secondhand impressions from talking with those who live and work in and around schools.

As stated in the Preface, this is not a research report. It is one person's impressions of conditions in our schools and of some trends in schooling that warrant serious analysis, reflection, and action. It is also one person's opinion of what schools should do.

This book is designed, most of all, to stimulate dialogue. If it provokes little more than a nod or a shake of the head — no impassioned agreement or disagreement — then I will have failed in my purpose. I think we have reached a critical juncture in American education and schooling. There is a lot of complaining and reacting but not enough thought about what we are doing and where we are going. We vacillate every few years from excessive attention to individuality to excessive attention to responsibility for our society's welfare. Education should cultivate both. Cremin succinctly states the problem and the need.

> How do we achieve the educational balance between individualism and community suggested in this [Dewey's] formulation . . . . We talk. The proper education of the public and indeed the proper creation of

publics will not go forward in our society until we undertake anew a great public dialogue about education. In fact, I would maintain that the questions we need to raise about education are among the most important questions that can be raised in our society, particularly at this juncture in our history. What knowledge should "we the people" hold in common? What values? What skills? What sensibilities? When we ask such questions, we are getting at the heart of the kind of society we want to live in and the kind of society we want our children to live in. We are getting at the heart of the kind of public we would like to bring into being and the qualities we would like that public to display. We are getting at the heart of the kind of community we need for our multifarious individualities to flourish.[2]

Chapter Two

On Social Purposes and Educational Goals

Loren Eisely once said that institutions are the bones of our civilization. They are created in response to the emergence of a need that must be met regularly and consistently. The desired response must not be left to chance and uncertainty.

Armies are created in anticipation of threats of war, police forces because crime is getting out of hand, banks when the direct bartering of goods becomes cumbersome, postal systems when face-to-face communication no longer is adequate, schools when the education needed is more than parents are able to provide. As new needs arise, existing institutions are called upon to do new things or new institutions are created. In the process, some institutions change so much that very little of what they once did remains. Some institutions change very little, even in the face of new demands, and continue for many more years before disappearing or being forced to change. Some institutions take on things that society never specifically nor officially asked them to do and things that they rarely include in citing their own functions.

One of the most interestingly complex needs to be met by any society is education. Education is not just a service to be encapsulated in an institution. It is far more pervasive than that, since it is a function of families, businesses, churches, and social clubs as well as schools, colleges, and universities. We live at a time when television has become a powerful educative force while its announced purpose is entertainment.

Education has a way of trickling out of any and all confinements, often to the annoyance of individuals and groups controlling various segments of society. Books are burned because they contain dangerous messages. The "Good Book" was retained in the hands of those who preached the Gospel until the printing press changed all that. Pages of books have been passed around as reminders of a cause gone underground.

Education given as acts of noblesse oblige to society's disadvantaged has come back full circle in the form of demands resulting from new insights and awareness derived from that same education. Little wonder that historically those in power often have feared education and sought to deny it or to provide inferior schooling to the masses. And little wonder that political coups customarily are followed by controls on schools and the modes and materials of instruction.

Just as education serves to close the gap between society's needs and society's goals, it also serves to push out the horizons of what could be. It is civilization's most significant process for determining what a society might become. It is also civilization's most exalted vehicle for getting there. In the U.S. and many other countries, this vehicle — education — and the institution of schooling are viewed virtually as one.

It is overly simplistic, but nonetheless useful, to suggest two different kinds of gaps between where a society is and where it might be. One is rather straightforward and calls for processes of social engineering; it is an engineering gap. A growing population requires more food; therefore, more land must be converted to agricultural purposes. The urbanization of that population calls for the construction of more housing. There is a job to do and the know-how for getting it done is available. Delays may occur because the funds have not yet been provided or because of political factors, but those who will do the job already have acquired most of the necessary training and skills. Goals are set, resources are mobilized, the job gets done; then attention shifts to some other gap requiring similar action.

The second kind of gap I call an education gap. This involves an awareness of improved conditions to be sought through the acquisition of more or better knowledge, beliefs, interests, skills, and ways of behaving on the part of as many people as possible. The education gap is the distance between man's most noble visions of what he might become and present levels of human functioning. It is a distance perceived by a large percentage of the people and it serves as a motivation for change and reform. When there are few visions beyond present preoccupations, when these preoccupations are narrowly self-indulgent, and when there is little societal self-consciousness of these conditions, then education is reduced to mere training for present pursuits. A society using its educational institutions and resources predominantly for training is in grave trouble.

It is important to make a clear distinction between gaps

requiring social engineering using the fruits of education and gaps requiring education that involves the long-term development of individual understandings and abilities. To make education into a vehicle for social engineering usually results in both disillusionment and the corruption of education. A short-term shortage of engineers is best met by providing special inducements for young adults to enter engineering, not by shifting the balance in the whole elementary and secondary curriculum toward science — a piece of logic we did not readily see in the late 1950s and early 1960s. If we see education as both the long- and the short-term answer to all of society's problems, we will make some grave errors in our use of schools.

In a primitive society the education gap is a narrow one; training suffices. Education is conducted largely through parental example; schooling, if any, is a short-term ceremony of induction rituals. Tradition and superstition prevail; religion takes on a very practical function by paying homage to the gods controlling the conditions of life — food, fire, water, and material safety. In such societies education is not a pressing concern. There is little need for school, that institution created to provide for needs not otherwise assured in the society.

In a complex, hierarchical society, expectations for segments of that society tend to be set in advance. Schools serve the social purpose of assuring that these expectations will be met. Schools may also serve to maintain the hierarchy. Going to school, not going to school, or going to certain kinds of schools may be more important for maintaining the hierarchy than what goes on in schools. The educating that does go on in them is carefully controlled through teacher education, materials of instruction, courses of study, and special mandates, monitored if not issued by local authorities. Social and communicative networks within the topmost levels of the hierarchy assure maintenance of career opportunities, privileges, and status for the favored class. Revolution is viewed by dissenters as the quick way to adjust inequities. Education is a much slower but ultimately more effective leveler. Schools, it often is charged, frequently are used to maintain the status quo rather than to educate in the true sense of that word.

In complex, hierarchical societies, as in primitive ones, tribal ceremonies of another sort are also important, especially for the more favored groups, which often increase the intensity of their rituals when their status is threatened. Reasoning frequently is tempered by class values and often is replaced by blind prejudice

17

when confronted with the rights and privileges of others. Religion serves as both a unifying and a divisive force, providing a common focus for worship but also reminding everyone that his or her status is God's will. Matters attributed to God's will are thus placed beyond rational, human intervention. To be content with one's lot is to follow God's will.

Education has a way of questioning and putting an end to much of this. Faith in God and the invocation of God's will to justify and sustain man's inhumanity to man are two very different things.

In a complex, relatively open society, opportunities and expectations for the individual are immensely diversified. Membership in groups depends less on family background and tradition and more on individual accomplishment and the ability to learn subtle cues. Successful persons usually move easily from group to group and are adept at taking on each group's special characteristics. Position, once established, is not guaranteed for life but may change dramatically because of job obsolescence, distinguished performance, fashion, errors in judgment, or changing political tides. There are many groups created to meet special needs and interests that exist because they provide satisfaction; membership in such groups is less and less dependent on inherited status, and they are less and less exclusive with respect to color, class, or creed.

The U.S. proudly proclaims that it is an open, classless society and often has sought to champion its system throughout the world. However, there is much yet to be done at home. A substantial gap continues to exist between our ideal visions and some present realities. This gap is in part an educational one.

The U.S. has looked to its educational system as a major contributing factor to its progress. Its public school system has been expected to provide the human resources for economic development as well as to prepare individuals who are capable of assuming many roles. Education and schooling have been equated, but in the process, education and training have been confused.

Faith in education and the transfer of that faith to our schools have contributed to an enormous expansion of our system of schooling, which in turn has taken on functions once performed by other institutions. Schooling has taken on (or been given) functions previously performed by the family. When a Gallup poll year after year shows discipline to be at the top of the list of parents' concerns about the schools, one wonders what this means regarding parental feelings of confusion, helplessness, and frustration in their own parenting role. The educating role of schools makes traditional aspects of family and church authority less "sacred." Much of what were once parents' inalienable rights or conditions attributed to God's will have become subject to critical inquiry. Schools that truly educate threaten long-standing mores and beliefs.

The humanization of knowledge or, put differently, the democratization of knowledge capital so that more and more people have access to it erodes the walls protecting privileges of birth and inheritance. There is considerable dispute among educational historians as to whether our schools have really democratized knowledge or whether schools have been maintaining a stratified social class structure. The respective arguments have been well advanced by others, and I do not intend to enter into them here. What is difficult to deny, I think, is that this country's massive experiment with universal elementary schooling and near-universal secondary schooling has resulted in an extraordinary distribution of knowledge capital. Further, the entire system of primary, secondary, and higher education, with all its shortcomings, has contributed to continuing unrest about human equality and justice.

Dynamic, developing societies depend in large measure on the maintenance of tension between the shortcomings of present realities and the promise of alternative possibilities, as well as on a willingness to close the gap. Where the gap is an educational one and is correctly perceived as such, attempts to close it open up new vistas and motivate fresh efforts toward human enlightenment and justice. A society advances through deliberately trying to improve itself. It becomes, ideally, fully educative in that the whole of life is examined. The process of improvement is not the prerogative of schools alone.

But when all of a society's problems and needs are perceived as an educational gap and education is equated with schooling, then schools are thrown into every breach. The educational system and the system of schooling become one and, as one, become "the foundation of our freedom, the guarantee of our future, the cause of our prosperity and power, the bastion of our security, the bright and shining beacon . . . the source of our enlightenment . . . ."[1] Schools become the instruments for more schooling, for career opportunities, for helping the disadvantaged attain first-class citizenship. As more and more people partake of what the system of schooling has to offer, the system loses for them some of its force as an instrument for tangible personal gain. When education has been for a long time equated with schooling and both are reduced to strictly instrumental values, schools and education are both discredited. When such disaffection is widespread, society itself is at a serious juncture.

Such a cycle can be documented in recent U.S. history. Following Sputnik, the schools were asked to provide the scientific muscle we needed for the dawning space age. Then they were to be the answer to urban decay, unemployment, and world tension. Meanwhile, they were to undergo a series of innovations in organization, curriculum, instructional materials, and teaching methods. Nothing was too much or too good for this "bastion of our civilization," the public school.

But there was a quick backlash to these inflated expectations. Expanded federal commitment to and more resources for schooling may have helped to fill an educational gap for the disadvantaged, but they did not produce the hoped-for upturn in urban conditions or a cure for other social ills. Social engineering, using all the know-how education has produced, is what the schools were asked to do. Education is the long, slow answer to civilization's problems. President Johnson was both right and wrong in his 1965 message to Congress.

Because too many people expected too much too soon from our schools, disillusion set in. This was not, however, disillusion solely over the school's apparent failure to cure social ills; its accomplishment of educational goals, too, was in question. Writing in 1970 about the general failure of supposed reforms in the 1960s, Peter Shrag began with the sentence, "It is 10 years later and the great dream has come to an end."[2]

The juncture to which we seem to have come raises the critical question as to whether our system of schooling has outlived its usefulness as an institution for both social reform and educational advancement. Critics may scoff at the way I have worded the previous sentence. Some would maintain that both claims are myths. I would have to nod in some agreement with those who say that schools tend to perpetuate many of the inequities of the surrounding society, that schools are weak agents of social reform, and that direct social reform and reconstruction of the schools must go hand in hand. And I would also have to nod in some agreement with those who say that our system of schooling has corrupted education. (I express my own deep concerns over this malaise later.)

The above arguments describe only one side of the coin,

however. I disagree especially with the deschooling solution to which such arguments often lead. The notion of a contemporary society without schools is not feasible, because we are not yet sufficiently advanced to educate through the whole culture, by *paedeia*. We have not yet harnessed other institutions or created the necessary new ones and charged them with educational responsibility. If we did not have schools, we would have to invent them. Perhaps we should proceed as though we were in the process of inventing them and ask ourselves, in this time and place, what schools are for.

While dreams for the Great Society and the role of education in ameliorating our social ills have been tempered markedly in recent years, there is ample evidence, nonetheless, to support the proposition that large numbers of young people, their parents, and other citizens still regard the lower schools as stepping stones to higher education and better career opportunities. Many of these people are in social groups who only recently began to believe (partly as a result of the successes of education and schooling) that these dreams might include them. They would like to believe that there will continue to be a system of public schooling and that schools will meet their expectations.

The assumed general dissatisfaction with schools warrants careful examination. Parents questioned in our in-depth study of 38 schools[3] gave high marks to their local schools. (These were not adults predominantly in the lower socioeconomic classes. As usual in efforts to secure such data, the sample reached in each school was skewed somewhat toward the more favored economically and the better educated.) These same respondents gave significantly lower marks to schools in general. Local schools fared less well with nonparents. Polls create public opinion as well as survey it. Have years of bad news about schooling convinced large numbers of people that "out there somewhere" are legions of bad schools?

If the local school remains relatively satisfactory in the eyes of those who send their children there, then that school already may have the support it needs for constructive change. To believe, however, that we can attain our ideals as a nation through community support for schools is akin to thinking that support for the local sheriff is an adequate answer to reducing crime. Our malaise runs deeper. It is not my intention to add a voice of doom to the many now being heard. This simply is one of those critical times in our history when it is necessary to reexamine long-

21

standing social purpose and get on with what it takes to achieve it. This means rethinking the role of all our institutions — among which schooling is but one, not sufficient to do the job alone but far too important to be ignored.

We confront two critical dangers. One is either not recognizing or not caring about the extraordinary gap between our noblest dreams and our present accomplishments, however impressive they may be according to some measuring sticks. The other is in corrupting education through both our limited conceptions of what it is and our readiness to accept what goes on in its name.

Our dreams have possessed a common, pervasive, and elusive quality, a promise of something unattained and yet attainable. The words always have come out the same: opportunity, freedom, prosperity, peace, and health and happiness for all. But some of our people know little of opportunity or freedom or health or happiness. And the world knows little of peace.

Millions have fallen far short of their potential by the simple fact of their birth. Born into impoverished families of sick, missing, or jobless parents, they have been able to claim only a meager share of the public schooling pronounced to be their birthright. These millions and more reveal that we are not yet the nation we aspire to be. These millions remind us, too, that they deserve something better for the most powerful of all reasons: They are human beings.

When it comes to enlightenment, creativity, and all those other qualities and sensibilities education is supposed to develop, who among us has achieved his or her full potential? How many of us, rich or poor, know the full meaning of man's humanity to man? How many of us think about the polluted waters, noxious air, ravaged land, and crumbling cities left in the wake of our march? Who among us possesses senses fully attuned to the sights, sounds, and smells of what nature has given and humans have created? Said the late Irwin Edman, "Life is for most of us what someone described music to be for the uninitiate: 'a drowsy reverie, interrupted by nervous thrills.' "

Unfulfilled social purpose and unrealized educational goals come together to remind us that schools, for as long as we have them, will be called upon to achieve social purposes while they educate. But, to repeat, not all social purposes are appropriate for schools, especially those calling only for training. Schools should take on only those social purposes that are most readily converted to educational goals.

Unfinished Social Purpose and Educational Goals

An example of how social purpose is converted to an educational goal is seen in the issue of desegregated schooling (social policy) and integration (educational goal). Prior to 1954, state and local education officials in many parts of the country saw little discrepancy, apparently, between segregated schools and the commonly articulated educational goal of "developing understanding and appreciation of all people, regardless of color, race, or creed." The Supreme Court's *Brown* decision in 1954 broke the states' legal sanctions justifying segregated schools and enunciated the school's role in a social purpose: Segregated schools are inherently unequal. Putting more resources into "separate but equal" schools could not change an inherently unequal condition. Schools were to be integrated.

Subsequent arguments for integration were predominantly educational ones: Blacks and other minorities would learn more, an argument at first bolstered by James Coleman's research. But the evaluative evidence was inconclusive. The hoped-for studies showing significant academic growth on the part of integrated, economically disadvantaged minorities in schools, even when supplemented by compensatory state and federal funds, did not come flowing in. The educational arguments for achieving social purpose were then thrown back into the faces of those who had used them. Why bus if the hoped-for educational advantages are little or none? Why break up an apparently successful all-black school where achievement test scores already exceed expectations?

The answer has been given many times but is not heard or is not liked when it is heard: Segregated schools are inherently unequal. Many school board members and other elected officials do not like to hear themselves saying it. But the courts hold firm. (Desegregated schooling's time would not yet have come if the courts had not and did not hold firm, illustrating again the school's limitations as an agent of reform unless strongly backed by other social institutions.)

Another example of the conversion of social purpose to educational goal, also dealing with segregation, is the education of the handicapped. Recent federal legislation, hailed as a bill of rights for the handicapped, mandates the mainstreaming of such children for their benefit and for the *benefit of other children*. Only time will tell whether the lofty social purpose of this legislation will be translated into educational goals that will benefit the handicapped and all other children.

The future of this country, it is argued, depends not just on desegregation but on the successful mixing of our diverse people. A nation of minorities cannot advance when they are walled off from each other. More than that, direct association is required if understanding, appreciating, and enjoying one another are to be cultivated through education. An old educational goal is dusted off and integration becomes its updated version.

This nation was born, the late James B. Conant once said, with a congenital deformity — second-class citizenship for some of its people. Just as the Supreme Court said that segregated schools are inherently unequal, second-class citizenship at birth is inherently unequal. The critical question is whether environmental intervention through education in our schools can overcome this congenital deformity. Certainly, the eradication of prejudice and racism is a legitimate educational goal, one to which we have given lip service for a long time and to which we must rededicate ourselves for a long time to come. But whether and how schools fulfill this goal as a function depends on the wisdom of our people — in effect, on whether our much-touted commitment to education reflects high aspirations or is a smokescreen for a variety of self-serving interests.

There are grounds for pessimism. Perhaps the most serious of these is that too many people simply will run away from our public educational system. They are justifiably concerned about the long trips required to bus children and youth to and from schools in the suburbs and the cities that would be almost all black or all white without such intervention. Magnet and other alternative schools are offered in some places as a palliative. One has the growing feeling during this period of limited school innovations that those few carried over from the 1960s would have less appeal if it were not for desegregation. Metropolitan plans, whereby school districts are rearranged so as to combine what are now suburban with urban districts, have tended to generate the most discontent over desegregation.

Private schools are commanding attention where there was little before. The voucher plan is another carry-over from the 1960s being looked at with fresh interest. There are elements of a limited voucher system that have educational appeal for me; I discuss them in the concluding chapter. But surely this must not be its time.

What too many people see in a voucher system during this time of stress for the public schools is part of what they and like-minded people seek in private schools. Put gently, it is a certain exclusiveness of association and community. I have many times asked friends and acquaintances why they send their children to private schools. Some genuinely believe that the education provided there is better. Almost all cite smaller classes. Most of the other reasons are from information provided by the schools' officials. (In a study of 201 nursery schools in the U.S., my colleagues and I were unable to identify better educational programs in the private ones, but we did identify significantly more and better self-congratulatory literature distributed to parents.)[4] When I push hard on whether these perceived advantages are worth paying for, especially given the strength of their own family backgrounds, a different kind of response surfaces. It has to do with the other families who send their children to Northrop Prep, the prestigious colleges attended by former graduates, the positions now held by alumni, and, indeed, the nice boys our daughters will meet. The private school network is one of several that add a margin of success to ability and help to offset its lack.

There is a role for private schools. It is largely one of setting an educational pace, breaking new ground, providing exemplary models for public schools to follow. Older readers may remember the outrage that followed James B. Conant's charge (while he was still president of Harvard) that in only a few isolated instances had private schools lived up to such a mission. Rather, he argued, their widespread existence in certain regions of the country, together with the concentration of leading families in them, weakened the fabric of support for the public schools and, indeed, our democracy.

Some major social purposes and educational goals enunciated both by our forefathers and by contemporary leaders have not been achieved. A public, tax-supported system of schooling has an important role to play in this extraordinarily important unfinished business. This role must be aided by those who have profited most from this nation's accomplishments to date. Many in these groups have been lulled into thinking that the job is done: Only the lazy and unmotivated go uncared for, and that is as it should be. Costly school programs should be cut back to the basics. Others are aware that part of our nation's business is unfinished but the future is one of limits; it is time to pull up the drawbridges. Give the people tax credits to shop for their children's education. Those who want something better and can afford it will find it in the best private schools.

These are not the views of a scattered few. Indeed, these

perspectives are broadly enough shared to endanger both our system of public schooling and the completion of important unfinished social purpose. Advocates of a voucher-based system of schooling view the times as propitious. Many citizens, however, regard with alarm what they see as movement away from the school system we have known. They argue for the neighborhood school concept, at the expense of desegregation through busing and metropolitan plans, to avoid white flight to private schools and self-selected alternative schools financed through vouchers. Some of these persons sincerely believe that the public school system must be preserved even if it means slowing down the integration process. Others simply use the argument to disguise their prejudice and racism.

No easy solution is in sight. Whatever the appeal of better education through a competitive voucher plan (and the evidence certainly is not available), too many people would embrace it for the wrong reasons. It is hard to imagine such a system advancing the social purposes of justice and equality to which this country is committed. To push strongly for achievement of such purposes through the public schools may drive more people out of the public schools. We can only hope that a core of dedicated citizens from all walks of life will hold fast, recognizing that we have weathered such storms before. The far greater acceptance of busing and other inconveniences of desegregation by children and youth, in contrast to their elders, provides grounds for encouragement.[5]

This is no time for abandoning commitment either to social purpose or public education. Rather, it is the very time for rededicating ourselves to public schools and their badly needed revitalization. More than this, we need to initiate a national dialogue about what education is, what it should do, and where it can be most productively advanced. To such a dialogue must be brought awareness of both the limitations of schools as agencies for direct social reform and the realization that schools must successfully ingest social purposes when these can be most readily converted to educational goals.

Diminished Educational Expectations

Contemporary scholar-critics denounce the schools on two counts: Schools have perpetuated the inequities of a class system (and been hypocritical in the process), and they have been miseducative. With two strikes like these, there is hardly need for a third! I have argued that the spread of knowledge capital through an expanding public school system has contributed to an awareness of the ideals to which we have aspired and has inspired many to keep striving toward them. There is no doubt in my mind that the schools must do a very much better job of educating if they are to be vital institutions in the future. Whether or not they can get better is a matter for serious conjecture, a matter that I examine later. Much depends on the education profession itself. Whether or not educators are up to what is required is a critical issue. But much depends, also, on the expectations and assumptions held by a significant portion of the surrounding culture. Society often gets what it deserves.

One popular assumption with profound implications for the goals of schooling is that schools went astray in the 1960s. Traditional content and teaching practices went out in an orgy of innovation that swept over every city and hamlet. There was, indeed, talk of reforms and a considerable flow of money. There were some changes, too, especially in materials of instruction. Undoubtedly, many teachers were disquieted by the admonition that they had to change their ways, but the inservice education and supportive infrastructure required for anything more than change at the periphery simply were not developed. Studies in the 1970s revealed that teaching practices in classrooms had gone relatively unmodified from preceding years. Most districts where substantial programs of reform had been under way for some years cut back as a spirit of counter-reform quickly mounted.

Nonetheless, during the 1970s we were told that we must get back to the basics; it was the will of the people. Or, was it actually a response to inflated rhetoric and another unexamined assumption? The 1977 Gallup Poll of the Public's Attitudes Toward the Public Schools revealed that 57% of those polled had never heard of the back-to-basics movement. Recent studies of schools and school districts suggest that parents have difficulty choosing among academic, social, vocational, and personal educational goals for their children. They want them all, at least for some stage of schooling. Statements promulgated at the state level, as we shall see in Chapter Three, include all four of these now-traditional sets of goals. State legislators during the 1970s, trying to define the fundamental goals and programs to be funded, usually came up with comprehensive statements that included the arts. Today there is little solid evidence to support the proposition that the American people, especially those with children in schools, want to turn back from those several broad goals that have emerged over the past three centuries.

Another assumption, implied in the charge that lowered SAT and other test scores were the bitter fruits of reforms occurring in the 1960s, is that the innovations of that decade were frivolous and irresponsible. Careful examination of the rationales underlying most of the innovations leads one to a quite different conclusion. At probably no other time in our history has there been an equivalent attempt to utilize extant knowledge and recent research about learners, learning, and subject matter to improve education. Rather than promulgating rote and passive learning, most of the reforms attempted to take into account decades of research into individual differences and the complexity of the learning process. Indeed, herein lay the seeds of failure. Teachers were asked to rise above many of the exigencies of limited classroom space and daily routine in an effort to make learning more meaningful, interesting, and dynamic. As stated earlier, the requisite inservice education and support structure were not usually provided. Teachers who did manage to rise to the challenge at times frequently dropped back to old routines requiring less expenditures of energy — and then were reinforced in this "return to normalcy" by the surge of back-to-basics rhetoric.

I regret to say that many educators are rather pleased to hear messages of diminished educational expectations for schools coming from others in the community. Not only do these messages imply simplistic approaches to teaching and learning but they also serve to sedate those troublesome pangs of a professional conscience which suggest that education is something more than animal-like training for tests of minimum proficiency. Even when these misguided messages are temporary, this does not get us around a formidable obstacle — namely, that the needed advances in school-based education are dependent on a relatively weak and divided profession that will be hard-pressed to effect the necessary breakthroughs on more than a limited front.

Another common and nonproductive assumption is that we know what goes on in schools and that we know what is required of the U.S. school system to set it right. Let me address the second half of this assumption first. Ours is a relatively loosely linked school system, organized state by state, that is surprisingly pervasive in its imposition of uniformities such as grades, daily schedules, and even pedagogical practices — sufficient to cause some historians to say, "A school is a school is a school." The drive to require minimum competencies for graduation from high school and even for grade-level promotion, accelerating during the second half of the 1970s, has resulted in even more state-by-state conformity.

Members of national commissions appointed to study schools usually assume not just these systemic commonalities but also a common school, and they formulate their recommendations accordingly. But is there such a thing? And, if there is, should there be? It is hard to believe that a three-room rural elementary school in Oklahoma is the same thing as a 30-room elementary school in any of our large cities or that it has the same meaning for the students. If they are a great deal alike, then perhaps this is the negative effect of systemic regularities and some drastic changes should be made. We are always exhorting visitors from abroad not to copy what may be quite inappropriate for them. And yet what they see in San Francisco may be more relevant to Brussels than to Burlington, Washington. Few recommendations directed at *the* American school are likely to address what any particular school most needs.

Turning to the first half of the assumption, none of the members of national commissions has an adequate diagnosis of what ails *the* American school, because there is no such thing. Few of those in and around a given local school are in a position to set an agenda for improvement, largely because they lack the data required for prescription. One of the reasons for this lack is an almost pathological preoccupation with standardized achievement test results, student marks, and evidences of order and discipline as criteria for school performance. Little evaluative attention goes to how students spend their time in school each day, what they study, whether they are bored or challenged, and whether they are being motivated to go on inquiring into themselves and civilization for the rest of their lives. Evidence regarding students' liking school and eagerly attending each day usually is rejected as soft and misleading.

These and many more are the kinds of data, gathered from 38 U.S. schools, that my colleagues and I are examining at the time this book goes to press. The purpose of our study is not to provide a report on the American school! Rather, it is to generate some fresh hypotheses regarding the nature of schools — their unique and common characteristics — and, more important, to highlight the importance of having such data for any school *before* setting priorities for its improvement. An ultimate outcome of our work will be, we hope, a comprehensive set of instruments for achieving such purposes.

Another assumption worth examining is that parents and other citizens are hungry to take over the operation of schools. Studies here and abroad reveal that parents want to be heard and, especially, to be kept well informed. But few appear to have the time and inclination required for more active involvement. They appear not to be distrustful of principals' and teachers' decisions. They do distrust decisions affecting their schools that are made in far-off places. In big cities, downtown often is a far-off place. Interestingly, a poll conducted during the late 1970s showed educators running far ahead of politicians in public trust and confidence. Is the education profession, with public support, capable of responding to that confidence with vastly improved school-based education?

Then there is the assumption that all would be well if parents did take over the schools. It is argued that they know what is best educationally for their children and merit both a wider range and greater freedom of choice. To question this assumption is to behave heretically. Nonetheless, I believe it to be pernicious. Let me hasten to add that I believe parents have a basic responsibility to educate themselves well regarding disease prevention, nutrition, and other aspects of parenting, including the school learning of their children — if only to protect themselves against inevitable professional abuses and shortcomings. But to expect them to create or choose wisely from "schools of choice" offering *real* alternatives is to make an array of assumptions that, for me, have dubious credibility. I would also question the ability of educators or parents to provide and sustain *real* philosophical and operational alternatives, school by school, and the desirability of doing so.

Do not our young people have a right to comprehensive educational programs in which they will experience and examine a variety of philosophical positions and not be denied access to some because of parental choice? And do not our young people have a right and an obligation to experience such programs in the company of a reasonably diverse sample of the human beings who make up this nation, however disposed their parents might be toward segregated schools? And does not the healthy future of this nation require both? What disturbs me most about unbridled parental authority and freedom to choose in matters pertaining to their children's education is the implied usurpation of the rights of children and youth not only to become intelligent decision makers but also to be assured adequate opportunity to be educated for a future their parents have not known and cannot predict.

Movement toward state mandated, precisely defined minimum competencies for school progress and high school graduation provides some unique twists to the issue of who is to be responsible and held accountable for the education of children and youth. If there are real choices and parental authority is supreme, then a large measure of accountability moves to parents. Quite apart from the fact that state actions increasingly make a mockery of parental rights, the fact that the states' definition of school-centered educational requirements are made very clear provides young people with a yardstick for measuring their own attainments. When they find themselves denied a high school certificate or a job requiring high-level mastery of competencies, who is the culprit? Does the young plaintiff sue the parent for choosing a poor alternative school? The school district for failing to provide an adequate range of choice? Or the state for infringing on his civil liberties through an ill-conceived, prejudicial definition of education?

And this brings me to the concluding assumption among all those warranting careful analysis if we are to make schools more educational: that schools are comparable to industrial plants and can be judged and improved using similar criteria and methods. Educational literature is replete with rejections of such comparisons but they persist, nevertheless. Perhaps one of the reasons we cannot rid ourselves of the model is our failure to come up with widely acceptable alternatives. Current interest in ethnographic, naturalistic studies of schools may give us some of the insights requisite to new models and theories.

The school-as-a-factory assumption is vulnerable from any of several critical perspectives. It is questionable that schools are goal-oriented in any directing, unitary sense. Making externally derived goals more precise doesn't necessarily make them guiding criteria for teachers, students, and parents. The factory/industrial model, even with its feedback loops, depends on a certain imperviousness to external pressures and disruptions. Even with the threat of collective bargaining to management, the three-year contract, nonetheless, guarantees some of the desired stability. Somewhat open at the ends, the model is virtually closed on the sides. Additional investment and know-how committed at the top have a good chance of showing up in the product and profits.

By contrast, the school is like a horse corral with most of the fences knocked down. Decisions about the diet of the horses and how their trainers are to behave are made in far-off places by people whose futures depend less on how the horses and trainers fare than on how their own images fare with a much larger audience of voters. A large part of this audience, in turn, owns stock in the horses but receives no quarterly dividend checks. And the money invested doesn't seem to result in better race tracks or faster horses.

So much for this primitive analogy. The point to be made is that the schools have several decision-making levels in the system and are open at top, bottom, and on all sides. A large number of the decisions made at the top (if decisions made at federal and state levels may be called the top) are irrelevant to the needs of particular schools and, if they get there at all, are twisted along the way or are neatly turned aside on arrival. Money and resources passed down to the schools are burdened with restraints regarding their use. The discretionary funds schools so badly require for their particular needs are seldom what they receive.

Furthermore, a school is not like a factory whose managers have the requisite resources and authority for making the decisions. Schools generally have neither the requisite resources nor the authority to be accountable for an end product. Accountability is a good word, and the concepts accompanying it are not to be taken lightly or turned aside by educators. But the approaches to accountability we have witnessed in recent years, which have assigned responsibility without any of the commensurate authority, are a sham. Unfortunately, such approaches have served, also, to undermine professionalism to the degree that raising the enthusiasm of teachers and securing their commitment for needed school reconstruction will be more difficult in the 1980s than in the 1960s.

The needed reconstruction is toward making schools more educational while they serve certain essential social purposes. If these purposes are too many and too grandiose, schools will have no sense of symmetry. Losing sight of their educational goals, they may pursue various activities hyperactively, but the education they provide probably will grow worse. This is, I suspect, what happened in the aftermath of the 1960s.

So long as we have schools, they will be called upon to serve social purposes. But they must not be regarded as the sole agent of social reform, nor as the scapegoat for the decline in society's ability to meet its challenges. As I have stated elsewhere:

Even in the best of circumstances the schools cannot meet these challenges alone, not while American society is in the midst of reappraising its place in the community of nations and reconsidering the ways its economic and political rewards are distributed . . . . These are issues that test the spirit, that call for leadership, that spring from our Constitution and history.[6]

The social purposes best served by schools are those most readily translated into educational goals. The educational goals for schools that have arisen largely out of emerging social needs in this country are discussed in Chapter Three. The chapter begins with a discussion of education — the condition and process to be fostered by schools if they are to warrant being designated as educational institutions.

Chapter Three

On Educational Aims and School Goals

Lawrence Cremin's succinct definition suggests the nature and scope of education: "[Education is] the deliberate, systematic, and sustained effort to transmit or evoke knowledge, attitudes, values, skills, and sensibilities."[1] Education occurs in the individual; it involves the whole of the individual; it occurs in schools, homes, churches, and other institutions as well as through the press, radio, and television.

Schools take on special significance because they and they alone were created to assure that a deliberate, systematic, and sustained process of educating would go on in our country. Other institutions such as the church continue to provide some specialized forms of education, but schools provide systematic general education. The purposes of a democracy require it. The needs of individuals make it essential.

Schools provide a public service, paid for out of public tax monies and in accord with people's willingness and ability to pay. Willingness and ability to pay fluctuate even when financial resources remain relatively constant. They are factors of satisfaction and perceived need that, together, determine what citizens are willing to pay for their schools. I recognize this to be an oversimplification of a relationship that does not operate so sensitively. The nature of the tax structure and institutionalized bureaucracy are such that tax revolts can occur before imbalances between services and demands for services are righted. Nonetheless, the point is clear: Our public system of schooling is to a considerable degree a servant to its clients and dependent for support upon their understanding of and belief in education.

Herein lies a paradox. Preceding chapters have emphasized the public's desire that education be practical. But the patrons of schools in our kind of society are impatient; they tend to want quick, highly tangible returns. State universities are ever being

34

called upon to justify themselves by demonstrating their contribution to improved agricultural methods, better oil refining methods, or the production of engineers. Their graduates are to possess employable skills. Curricula and enrollments are more responsive to the job market and the economy than to considerations of what constitutes the educated person.

Much of the educating required by the job market could be better and more efficiently done by businesses and industries — and often is. But why should they go to this expense if job preparation can be done by schools, colleges, and universities? One of the major problems for all educational institutions is how they can satisfy the demands of their clients and still educate. The balance is a precarious one.

What makes the balance particularly delicate is the fact that education, properly conducted, *is* eminently practical. It prepares not for just one but many vocations; it prepares not just for society as it is but for a changing civilization; it provides not merely for present satisfactions but makes possible a lifetime of enjoyment. What could be more practical? The distinction between educating and training is as much one of style as of specifics. The distinction has gone seriously awry when we speak of being "overeducated." David S. Saxon says:

> Let's examine this curious new term, overeducation. Overeducation for *what*? Too much learning for a full and satisfying life? Too much schooling for a lifetime of changing careers in a rapidly changing world? Too much education for active participation in the affairs of a modern democratic government?
>
> To the extent that the level of education and society's ability to put it to use are presently out of balance, then what a peculiarly negative solution — what a tragic waste of human potential — to limit education and learning. Wouldn't it make far better sense to concentrate on how to use the full capacity of all of our citizens?
>
> I think we are more in need of wisdom today than at most earlier stages in our history. A broad liberal education is not the only ingredient of wisdom, but it is an essential one. We need all the knowledge we can muster to meet our technological and scientific problems. We need all the accumulated experience and understanding of humanity we can absorb to meet our social problems. And I believe we can ill afford the risk of foreclosing the maximum cultivation of that knowledge and understanding simply because it seems not to be required for immediate vocational purposes.[2]

Dewey recognized and spoke out for the importance of vocational competency. But he saw the danger, as Saxon clearly states it above, of training for specific vocational ends. Dewey expressed his concern about acceptance of the status quo, not only for industry but also for societies full of inequities, when he said:

> Wherever social control means subordination of individual activities to class authority, there is danger that industrial education will be dominated by acceptance of the status quo. Differences of economic opportunity then dictate what the future callings of individuals are to be. We have an unconscious revival of the defects of the Platonic scheme without its enlightened method of selection.[3]

This duality, society vs. the individual, has been a philosophical issue in education for centuries. Presumably, Plato was reacting in part to challenges to the authority of the state by excessive individualism when he wrote *The Republic*. He proposed an ideal state characterized by unity and harmony to which citizens, thinking of themselves as an integral part of the state, would give loyalty and obedience. Developing individuals to their fullest potential often has been argued as the antithesis of educating the individual to serve the state in the Platonic scheme of things. Nonetheless, some of the qualities Plato sought through the education of individuals and the kinds of studies he considered appropriate are not unlike those recommended by philosophers much less interested in having education serve the state as its first priority.

But what some object to is the degree to which schools are charged with instilling values the state deems inviolable. They see contradictory tendencies in the dual aims of education and no easy blending of individual and societal needs. Whatever the schools may be able to accomplish in promoting literacy, critical thinking, and cultural enlightenment, they are simultaneously required to instill a sense of devotion to the nation-state. Educational rhetoric may stress the cultivation of individual autonomy and independence, but in practice such efforts usually stop somewhat short of the point where allegiance and devotion to the state are challenged or training for the requirements of the state is threatened. Neither the individual potential for personal excellence nor the human ability to create a better civilization should be thus curtailed. There must be no duality, then, in the aims of education. The making of free individuals will result in the making of a free, democratic state. In this we must have faith or education will be corrupted.

Dewey entered into this dialectic at a time when those virtues believed to be inherent in the founding of this country and the cause of much of its subsequent progress had been translated into precepts to be taught in the schools. Dewey would not necessarily have quarreled with these; they simply were irrelevant to his theory of education. The aims of education, according to Dewey, are found within the process, not outside it in the state. The state does not set the aims of education, nor do its educational pronouncements have any immunity from critical examination through the educational process. It is one's individual observations and judgments that count in a continuous striving to improve the quality of one's experience and, therefore, one's life.

Heretical views for early twentieth-century America! They aroused many to fury.

Dewey contributed significantly to the concept of educating for self-realization. Rhetoric and practice in the early years of the twentieth century and before had stressed education for responsibility — to God, country, home, and job. Cremin paraphrased Dewey's definition of education — the reconstruction or reorganization of experience — as "a way of saying that the aim of education is not merely to make citizens, or workers, or fathers, or mothers, but ultimately to make human beings who will live life to the fullest."[4]

Dewey's notion of aims being found within the educational process does not mean that he rejected the idea of ends. On the contrary, he held two distinctly different concepts of ends. The first is end as the final activity in a sequence, with or without any sense of purpose. The second is end-in-view, that is, an expectation of something to occur, whether or not it ever does. But Dewey's end-in-view was not necessarily a precise objective to be attained; indeed, it could be a process that would have certain qualitative characteristics. The distinction between ends-in-view and means-to-an-end becomes obscure. Assigning an instrumental role to means and evaluating them according to achievement of ends-in-view becomes difficult if not impossible.

R.S. Peters goes even further in setting aims within the context of educating:

> I have argued elsewhere that much of the confusion about "aims in education" comes about through extracting the normative feature built into the concept of "education" as an extrinsic end. Given that "education" suggests the intentional bringing about of a desirable state of mind in a morally unobjectional manner, it is only too easy to conceive of education as a neutral process that is instrumental to something that is worthwhile which is extrinsic to it. Just as gardens may be cultivated in order to aid the economy of the household, so children must be educated in order to provide them with jobs and to increase the productivity of the community as a whole.

But there is something inappropriate about this way of speaking; for we would normally use the word "train" when we had such a specific extrinsic objective in mind. If, however, we do specify an appropriate "aim" such as the development of individual potentialities or the development of intellect and character, then the aim would be intrinsic to what we would consider education to be.[5]

There can be no serious discussion of what education is for, then, without that discussion embracing what education is. Similarly, there can be no serious consideration of what schools are for without simultaneously considering what education is. To evaluate schooling solely for its contribution to specific goals and objectives is to misinterpret what education is all about. As Dewey said:

Since growth is the characteristic of life, education is all one with growing; it has no end beyond itself. The criterion of the value of school education is the extent to which it creates a desire for continued growth and supplies means for making the desire effective in fact.[6]

Education, then, is a process of individual becoming. The aim of education is to have this process occur or, better, to have it flourish. The essence of the process is the growth taking place in the individual and the meaning of that growth for the individual. The richer that meaning, the more it creates a desire for continued growth and the better the quality of the educational experience.

Evaluation of the process is faced with two challenges. The first involves the extraction and interpretation of personal meaning. But since meaning is individual to the learner, the evaluator must become an agent in the individual's reconstruction of the experience. It is easy to see why this first challenge has been largely ignored in the evaluation of school-based education. If it is to be met at all, it must be in the role of teachers — a role that, regrettably, few are well prepared to undertake.

The second evaluative challenge is that of determining the ways in which and the extent to which educational programs encourage and support personal growth and motivate the desire for more. If the meanings being derived from experience with the educational activities are self-deprecating, then drastic changes must be made. As Whitehead says in *The Aims of Education*, "Primarily it is the schools and not the scholars which should be inspected."[7] This challenge simply has been sidestepped for something much simpler. Goals articulated by the state are substituted for personal growth, and the quality of educational programs is then judged according to levels of goal attainment.

Programs need not be examined at all!

For this kind of evaluative process to be conducted "scientifically," the state's goals for its schools are broken down into detailed behavioral objectives. It is a large leap from the former to the latter. What evidence do we have that any eight or 10 or 50 behavioral objectives, even if attained, add up to some larger traits of the kind implied in educational aims since the time of Aristotle or, for that matter, state or locally prescribed goals? The answer is, of course, very little. Following the earlier quote from Peters, the mistake is in trying to extract the norms built into the educational process and encapsulate them in extrinsic goals to be achieved. On this and other corruptions of education I have more to say in Chapter Four.

It is interesting that, in his *The Aims of Education,* Whitehead does not begin with goals or directions. He begins with the place of ideas in teaching: They should be few and important; they should be interconnected (the role of theory); the child should make them his own (the joy of discovery). The closest he gets to a sense of specific direction is the following: "What we should aim at producing is men who possess both culture and expert knowledge in some special direction."[8] He then goes into what is essentially a differentiation between general and specialized education — the problem of producing the expert without loss of the virtues of the amateur — and with a definition of style as the last acquisition of the educated mind. "Style is the ultimate morality of mind . . . the exclusive privilege of the expert."[9]

It should come as no surprise that Whitehead's further elaboration, in a related essay, eschews no separation of ends and means. Rather, he addresses the rhythm and character of mental growth and the importance of being attuned to it in teaching. From the nature of this rhythmic development, he conveys the qualities of romance, precision, and generalization that are to characterize three successive educational stages. "Education should consist in a continual repetition of such cycles."[10]

Let me pause now to summarize three essential points: First, the expectations of those who support schools and the dependence of schools on their clients can lead only too easily to the corruption of education for purposes of training. Second, a classic duality in the aims of education too often leads to the imposition of external goals on a process that can only occur in individuals and that has its own intrinsic norms. These two points in no way should be taken to imply that education and schooling are devoid of responsibility to a larger social order. But an important perspective is involved — that cultivation of an individual sense of responsibility is the best assurance of a sound, moral social order. Norman Cousins presents the perspective succinctly:

> If the main purpose of a university is job training, then the underlying philosophy of our government has little meaning. The debates that went into the making of American society concerned not just institutions or governing principles but the capacity of humans to sustain those institutions. Whatever the disagreements were over other issues at the American Constitutional Convention, the fundamental question sensed by everyone, a question that lay over the entire assembly, was whether the people themselves would understand what it meant to hold the ultimate power of society, and whether they had enough of a sense of history and destiny to know where they had been and where they ought to be going.[11]

Third, the norms for judging the quality of education being provided by schools or any other educational institutions are found in the context, the programs and the processes, where the activities presumed to be educative occur. This does not rule out accountability and the evaluation required for judging the quality of this context. But it turns attention to the norms or values inherent in the activities and, therefore, to the need for appraising these activities according to criteria other than or in addition to goals. Even when one concedes the importance of goals for schooling — and one must — it is the quality of the activities of schooling that will determine the degree to which schools are educative. Robert Rosen observes that:

> . . . man has a biologically rooted need to engage in complex activities . . . . And it is the activities themselves which are needful, not the ends to be attained by them; these ends are the inessentials and the by-products. Somehow, we have gotten turned around so as to believe that, on the contrary, the ends are primary and the means secondary.[12]

From School Goals to Educational Programs

In previous chapters I have raised the question of the school's ability to convert social purpose to educational goal. The prime example used was the conversion of desegregation as social policy to integration as educational goal. In this chapter I have introduced the problem of schools being educative while achieving certain social goals.

In effect, I have turned the conventional question around. Instead of asking how schools are to achieve the educational goals set for them, I am asking how schools can be educative while seeking to achieve the goals set for them. So conceived, goals become not only ends to be reckoned with outside of the educational process but also norms not necessarily compatible with "the normative feature built into the concept of 'education.' " Put negatively, the question becomes, "How do schools keep from corrupting education while pursuing their goals?" More positively, it becomes, "How do schools advance education while accounting for the goals society sets for them?"

A definition of education stressing personal growth, the desire for further growth, and the understanding of what is required for that growth does not lend itself to a neat means-ends model of how schools should improve their performance. And because of the dominance of the production model of schooling with ends being defined without consideration of the process, it is difficult even to think about schools achieving goals that are not derived from empirical tests of efficient goal attainment. Prevailing "rationality" defines good means as those that produce the desired outcomes; better means are those that produce them more efficiently. How beguilingly sensible!

The process of infusing educational concepts into the system of schooling begins, then, with the goals articulated for that system. The logical inference from the discussion of educational aims in the first section of this chapter is that such goals should be abolished or ignored. Schools probably would be more educative as a result. There is not in this country a set of goals articulated for universities for which they are to be held accountable. Such would be considered an infringement on academic freedom and institutional prerogative.

There are no signs, however, that states are about to abolish goals for schooling; schools must cope with them. Indeed, state legislators and educational leaders are fascinated with the prospect of reducing general goals to such specificity that there will be no mistaking what is required to achieve them, measure them, and make teachers and students alike accountable for achieving them. Decades ago Franklin Bobbitt enthusiastically demonstrated how this reductionism, carried far enough, virtually determines the curriculum.[13]

And this is precisely what is wrong with the process. *It is the very generality of educational goals that protects them against abuse and leaves room for the advancement of education in schools and classrooms.*

It may surprise the reader for me to say that I have no objection to the occasional use of behavioral objectives *as a pedagogical device.* So used, behavioral objectives become an

41

alternative way or means and not ends at all, useful on some occasions but not on others. And when they are used, they can be subjected to empirical test like any other method.

But when such objectives are set up outside of the educational process as ends to be achieved and measured and then used as criteria for judging the merits of *other* means, a mischief is perpetrated. This alternative pedagogical technology is placed outside the domain of empirical scrutiny and declared the norm.

My quarrel with behavioral reductionism, then, is its application to the supposed clarification of ends and the ultimate deification of means as ends. A keen eye must also be turned to limits on the applicability of behavioral objectives to means within the familiar means-ends model of appropriateness and efficiency. The body of supporting evidence for teaching by the reduction of ends-in-view to precise behavioral objectives is not convincing. While much of the available research supports the observation that students appear to achieve objectives better when teachers define them better (that is, more precisely), such a conclusion must be taken with a large grain of tautological salt. This is like saying that students are more likely to run in straight lines when asked or required to do so. And, again, the objective, once precisely defined, now achieves validity as the norm and is put outside the scrutiny of empirical inquiry.

Better research examines the use of precisely defined behavioral objectives appropriately as means and concludes that the practice works better for some learnings than for others — a not uncommon finding in the pedagogical arena. Not surprisingly, the simpler the learning task (counting or kicking a ball), the more productive the practice of using precisely defined objectives. But the more complex the task and the more it calls for original, creative thinking, the less useful is the process of step-by-step behavioral reduction.

Ralph Tyler often has been called the father of behavioral objectives and is credited or maligned, according to one's point of view. He most certainly employed the term. But reading his basic work in the curriculum field[14] suggests that he had in mind something quite different from the long lists of behavioral competencies currently found in curriculum writing or the lists of proficiencies now frequently required for student promotion or graduation. He even cautioned against the formulation of more than 15 categories, because of the pedagogical difficulties presented by a larger number, a caveat borne out by some subsequent research. His examples of how these might be defined could hardly satisfy today's advocate of behavioral objectives. Tyler's categories are: the acquisition of information; the development of work habits and study skills; effective ways of thinking; social attitudes, interests, appreciations, and sensitivities; the maintenance of physical health; and the development of a philosophy of life.[15]

He appeared to have at least two reasons for maintaining this level of generality and as much discreteness as possible between categories. First, he apparently thought it important for the faculty members of a secondary school or an English department to engage in dialogue about the meaning of a goal for them. Precise predefinition could only be arbitrary, restrictive, and ultimately dysfunctional. Second, as a behavioral scientist, he was aware that different kinds of human behavior are acquired in different ways. Consequently, some general differentiation of types of behavior implied some differentiation in learning and pedagogical approach at the classroom level:

> Other things being equal, more general objectives are desirable rather than less general objectives. However, to identify appropriate learning experiences it is helpful to differentiate rather clearly types of behavior which are quite different in their characteristics. Hence, one can sharply differentiate such a behavioral classification as the acquisition of facts which may be viewed primarily as memorization and the ability to apply principles to new problems which involves primarily the interpretation and use of facts and principles. On the other hand, some headings fall in between; for example, understanding important facts and principles implies memorization — one knows what they are and can state them — but it also implies more than sheer memorization; it implies some ability to indicate the meaning, some ability to suggest illustrations of these facts and principles, and, in a limited sense, some ability to apply them to other situations.[16]

It is easy to see, of course, how Tyler's differentiation of types of behavior provides a launching pad for rampant reductionism. What has been ignored almost entirely in his position, however, is his concern with what he called "the content aspects in the satisfactory formulation of objectives." Content was to be selected not just to achieve an objective but to assure that the major domains of human experience were included in the education of students.

The question of what knowledge is of most worth becomes an integral part of curriculum planning. It is not enough to understand facts and principles. The question is: What facts and principles? It is not enough to learn a behavior well. The question is: What behaviors are worth learning?

Educational Aims and School Goals

By the mid-1970s such questions were regarded in many quarters as quaint and archaic, or were simply ignored as irrelevant. Whereas during the 1960s considerable energy and money went into determining the substance of the curriculum and methods of instruction, the energy of the 1970s was consumed with power struggles,[17] involving refinement of the behavioral bases of accountability and development of tests for measuring attainment of defined competencies and proficiencies. One could only hope that this period of low regard for what is basic and central to education was preliminary to a renaissance of interest in classic questions of curriculum, learning, and teaching.

The beginning of such a renaissance might very well lie in a dialogue about the extant goals for schooling that have emerged in this country over a period of more than three hundred years. Rather than reducing such goals to hundreds or thousands of specific behaviors, we should seek to understand their meaning for substance and process — in effect, to determine whether and how they might be advanced through educating. Or, to put it differently, we should inquire into whether and how these goals and education might be advanced simultaneously.

Goals for schooling emerge through a sociopolitical process in which certain sets of interests prevail over others for a period of time. These are client-perceived wants and needs, professional determinants (such as those of subject-matter organizations), pervasive interests of the citizenry in teaching a common culture, expectations of colleges and universities, and the economic interests of business and industry and of the nation as a whole.[18] The goals that have emerged in the U.S. may be placed conveniently into four categories: 1) academic — early emphasis was on sufficient schooling to learn the principles of religion and the laws of the land (sometimes defined as functional literacy); 2) vocational — readiness for productive work and economic responsibility; 3) social and civic — socialization for participation in a complex society; 4) personal — the goal of personal fulfillment, which is a fairly recent development.

These categories have usually been kept in rhetorical balance until the threat of war, a declining economy, or perceived excesses in prevailing practices precipitate special investigations (white papers, Presidential panels, etc.) and reform efforts. Accompanying debate usually sets up a dichotomy between responsibility to an ever-widening social and cultural order and development of the individual. The pendulum subsequently

44

swings (at least rhetorically) toward one or the other of these dual thrusts.

In any examination of goals articulated for schools, a central consideration is the comprehensiveness of the total list and the balance of interests inherent in it. In any examination of schools themselves, a central consideration is the comprehensiveness of the program and the balance inherent in it.

Data gathered from the sample of students, teachers, and parents in schools selected for A Study of Schooling (referred to in Chapters One and Two) support the importance of all four categories of goals listed above. Although teachers and parents of elementary school children rated vocational education somewhat below the other three categories of goals in importance, teachers, parents, and secondary school students thought that all four *should* be "very important" at school.[19]

In the early, conceptual stage of A Study of Schooling, several colleagues[20] and I engaged in an analysis of goals for schooling articulated by state and local boards of education, various special commissions, and others in an attempt to achieve a synthesis. From approximately 100 such goals, we ultimately defined 12 that seemed to constitute a reasonably discrete list with a minimum of repetition; all were at about the same level of generality. To the degree possible, we tried to retain the original linguistic nuances and emphases; needless to say, the process of refinement resulted in some loss.

Viewed historically, the goal statements reflect both some concern for the times and for social purposes designed to remedy a condition or to produce a more desired one. Over time, shifts have occurred. The shift in the U.S. over more than three centuries has been from discipline honed by the classics and religion to civic, religious, and vocational responsibility; to worthy membership in home, community, state, and nation; to concern for justice and respect for others; to appreciation for democratic values; to respect for self and development of individual talents.

On succeeding pages I present the 12 goals that emerged from our analysis, employing as much of the original language as we were able to preserve. The subdivisions under each heading provide a variety of perspectives on what is meant by each of the abbreviated headings. The short paragraph following each list of subdivisions provides a rationale for the goal. As noted, we preserved as many as possible of the initial nuances.

I present the list in its entirety because it provides, I think, a reasonably accurate and comprehensive summary of our verbal (and, to a considerable degree, our ideal) commitment to goals for schooling. Broadly representative of interests, the 12 goals constitute a sociopolitical expression of external expectations to which school personnel presumably are to pay some attention and for which they might expect to be held accountable. The list corresponds rather closely to those prepared during the late 1970s by various states, sometimes under the rubric of "basic education."

Those legislators, school board members, and educators who sought, for whatever reason, to define basic education as "basic skills and fundamental processes" should readily see how far afield they were in selecting just one category from the range of goals to which we presumably are committed as a nation. It is regrettable — indeed reprehensible — that so many educators settle for so impoverished a conception of education when it appears expedient to do so. As Whitehead expressed it, "When one considers in its length and breadth the importance of a nation's young, the broken lives, the defeated hopes, the national failures, which result from the frivolous inertia with which it [education] is treated, it is difficult to restrain within oneself a savage rage."[21]

The list is presented here to serve, also, as a beginning point in a dialogue about education and what schools are for that should be going on in this nation and especially among school-community groups and the total faculties of individual schools. There is no need to begin from scratch, as most such dialogues do, on the assumption that we have no goals for schooling. Rather, we should be addressing ourselves to such questions as the meaning and significance of such goals, their implications for educational practice, and whether or not we intend to carry out what these goals seem to imply.

Goals for Schooling in the U.S.

1. Mastery of basic skills or fundamental processes
    1.1 Develop the ability to acquire ideas through reading and listening
    1.2 Develop the ability to communicate ideas through writing and speaking
    1.3 Develop the ability to understand and utilize mathematical concepts
    1.4 Develop the ability to utilize available sources of information

1.5 Develop the ability to read, write, and handle basic arithmetical operations

In our technological civilization, an individual's ability to participate in the activities of society depends on mastery of these fundamental processes. The level of verbal and mathematical literacy required is one that will enable individuals to apply and utilize these basic skills in the varied functions of life. With few exceptions, those who are deficient in basic skills will be severely limited in their ability to function effectively in our society.

2. Career education-vocational education
   2.1 Develop the ability to select an occupation that will be personally satisfying and suitable to one's skills and interests
   2.2 Develop salable skills and specialized knowledge that will prepare one to become economically independent
   2.3 Develop attitudes and habits (such as pride in good workmanship) that will make the worker a productive participant in economic life
   2.4 Develop positive attitudes toward work, including acceptance of the necessity of making a living and an appreciation of the social value and dignity of work

Within the structure of our present society, an individual will spend a large portion of his time working. Therefore, an individual's personal satisfaction will be significantly related to satisfaction with his job. In order to make an intelligent career decision, he needs to know his own aptitudes and interests as they relate to career possibilities. Next, he must be able to obtain whatever specialized training is necessary to pursue the vocation selected and to develop attitudes that will help him succeed in his field. This goal is important not only for the individual's satisfaction but also for the continued growth and development of society.

3. Intellectual development
   3.1 Develop the ability to think rationally; i.e., thinking and problem-solving skills, use of reasoning and the application of principles of logic, and skill in using different modes of inquiry
   3.2 Develop the ability to use and evaluate knowledge; i.e., critical and independent thinking that enables one to make judgments and decisions in a wide variety

of life roles (e.g., citizen, consumer, worker, etc.) as well as in intellectual activities

    3.3 Accumulate a general fund of knowledge, including information and concepts in mathematics, literature, natural science, and social science

    3.4 Develop the ability to make use of knowledge sources, utilizing technology to gain access to needed information

    3.5 Develop positive attitudes toward intellectual activity, including intellectual curiosity and a desire for further learning

As civilization has become increasingly complex, man has had to rely more heavily on his rational abilities. Today's society requires the full intellectual development of each member. This process includes not only the acquisition of a fund of basic knowledge, but also the development of basic thinking skills. Only those individuals with the ability to think rationally and logically, to make critical judgments, and to utilize past knowledge as well as the rapidly expanding fund of new information to solve problems will be active and effective participants in the society of the present and the future.

   4. Enculturation

    4.1 Develop insight into the values and characteristics of the civilization of which one is a member

    4.2 Develop awareness of one's cultural and historical heritages — the literary, aesthetic, and scientific traditions of the past — and familiarity with the ideas that have inspired and influenced mankind

    4.3 Develop understanding of the manner in which heritages and traditions of the past are operative today and influence the direction and values of society

    4.4 Acquire and accept the norms, values, standards, and traditions of the groups of which one is a member

    4.5 Examine the norms, values, standards, and traditions of the groups of which one is a member

A study of traditions that illuminate our relationship with the past can yield insight into our present society and its values. Moreover, an individual's sense of belonging to a society is strengthened through an understanding of his place in that tradition, while the record of human aspiration may suggest direction for his own life. All these perceptions will contribute to the development of the individual's sense of identity.

5. Interpersonal relations
   5.1 Develop a knowledge of opposing value systems and their influence on the individual and society
   5.2 Develop an understanding of how members of a family function under different family patterns
   5.3 Develop skill in communicating effectively in groups
   5.4 Develop the ability to identify with and advance the goals and concerns of others
   5.5 Develop the ability to form productive and satisfying relations with others based on respect, trust, cooperation, consideration, and caring
   5.6 Develop an understanding of the factors that affect social behavior

Rapid personal and social change is taking place in today's society. Human beings are subjected to new and increasingly fragmented roles. In a complex, interdependent world, individual mental health is closely related to the larger social structure — to one's interpersonal relations. No one goes unaffected by the actions of other people. The individual or nation that pursues a mindless, self-indulgent course offends the sensibilities, endangers the health, or threatens the lives of others. Understanding oneself is not enough — one must transcend self to become aware of and to understand all people and their institutions, all nations and relations, all cultures and civilizations — past, present, and future. Schools should help every child to understand, appreciate, and value persons belonging to social, cultural, and ethnic groups different from his own; and to increase affiliation and decrease alienation.

6. Autonomy
   6.1 Develop a positive attitude toward learning
   6.2 Develop skill in selecting personal learning goals
   6.3 Develop skill in coping with and accepting continuing change
   6.4 Develop skill in making decisions with purpose
   6.5 Develop the ability to plan and organize the environment in order to realize one's goals
   6.6 Develop the willingness to accept responsibility for and the consequences of one's own decisions

Schools that do not produce self-directed citizens have failed both society and the individual. Adults unable to regulate and guide their own conduct are a liability to society and themselves. As a society becomes more complex and less absolute, more relative, more ambiguous, and less structured, demands upon the individual multiply. We have created a world in which there no longer is a common body of information that everyone must or can learn. The only hope for meeting the demands of the future is the development of people who are capable of assuming responsibility for their own needs. Schools should help every child to prepare for a world of rapid change and unforeseeable demands in which continuing education throughout his adult life should be a normal expectation.

7. Citizenship
   7.1 Develop a sense of historical perspective
   7.2 Develop knowledge of the basic workings of the government
   7.3 Develop a commitment to the values of liberty, government by consent of the governed, representational government, and responsibility for the welfare of all
   7.4 Develop an attitude of inquiry in order to examine societal values
   7.5 Develop the ability to think productively about the improvement of society (refer to No. 3)
   7.6 Develop skill in democratic action in large and small groups (refer to No. 5)
   7.7 Develop a willingness to participate in the political life of the nation and community
   7.8 Develop a commitment to the fulfillment of humanitarian ideas everywhere
   7.9 Develop a commitment to involve oneself in resolving social issues

More than ever before, man is confronted with confusion regarding the nature of man; conflicting value systems; ambiguous ethical, moral, and spiritual beliefs; and questions about his own role in society. There is a major struggle over the issue of whether man is for government or government is for man. The question is not whether there should be some form of government, but what are its roles, functions, structures; and what are its controls? There is now earlier involvement of youth in politics and national life, and there are demands by minorities for greater access to power in our country. To counteract man's ability to destroy himself and his tendency to destroy his environment requires citizen involvement in the political and social life of this country. A democracy can only survive by the participation of its members.

8. Creativity and aesthetic perception

   8.1 Develop the ability to motivate oneself, to deal with new problems in original ways

   8.2 Develop the ability to be sensitive to problems and tolerant of new ideas

   8.3 Develop the ability to be flexible, to redefine skills, and to see an object from different points of view

   8.4 Develop the ability to enjoy and be willing to experience the act of creation

   8.5 Develop the ability to understand creative contributions of others and to evaluate them

   8.6 Develop the ability to communicate through creative work in an active way (as a creator) or a perceptive way (as a consumer)

   8.7 Develop the commitment to enrich cultural and social life

The ability of the individual to create new and meaningful things and to appreciate the creations of other human beings is essential both for personal self-realization and for the benefit of human society. In spite of the fact that the measurement of creative processes and products is far from being satisfactory, there is general agreement among educators on the importance of developing the creative abilities of the student in the realms of both art and science.

9. Self-concept

   9.1 Develop the ability to search for meaning in one's activities

   9.2 Develop the self-confidence needed for confronting one's self

   9.3 Develop the ability to live with one's limitations and strengths

   9.4 Develop both general knowledge and interest in other human beings as a means of knowing oneself

   9.5 Develop an internal framework by which an individual can organize his concept of "self"

   9.6 Develop a knowledge of one's own body and a positive attitude toward one's own physical appearance

The self-concept of an individual serves as a reference point for nearly all of his activities. Individuals develop their personal goals and aspirations by using their self-concept as a feedback mechanism. There is no direct way of teaching the student to

51

develop a positive self-concept, but there are facilitating factors that could be provided in the school environment.

10. Emotional and physical well-being
    10.1 Develop the willingness to receive new impressions and to expand affective sensitivity
    10.2 Develop the competence and skills for continuous adjustment and emotional stability
    10.3 Develop the ability to control or release the emotions according to one's values
    10.4 Develop the ability to use leisure time effectively
    10.5 Develop positive attitudes and habits toward health and physical fitness
    10.6 Develop physical fitness and psychomotor skills

The emotional stability and the physical fitness of the student are perceived as necessary conditions for attaining the other objectives, but they can be viewed also as ends in themselves, stressing emotional sensitivity and empathy for fellow man and expression of emotions for the sake of creativity.

11. Moral and ethical character
    11.1 Develop the judgment to evaluate events and phenomena as good or evil
    11.2 Develop a commitment to truth and values
    11.3 Develop the ability to utilize values in determining choices
    11.4 Develop moral integrity
    11.5 Develop an understanding of the necessity for moral conduct
    11.6 Develop a desire to strengthen the moral fabric of society

Society, religion, and philosophy serve as guideposts for moral conduct. The individual is expected to control his behavior according to one or several systems of values. Models for some of these values are implicit in other persons' behavior (parents, teachers, state leaders), and other values are manifested in the form of a moral code.

12. Self-realization
The ideal of self-realization is based on the idea that there is more than one way of being a human being and that efforts to develop a better self contribute to the development of a better society.

Commentary

In using the foregoing list as a catalyst for discussing what schools are for, I now raise several distinctly different kinds of questions, using some of the goal statements as illustrations. One of my purposes is to get beyond the too-common practice of separating out and refining, *ad infinitum,* behavioral components of goal statements as though no other kinds of considerations were involved in educating.

Goal 2, "vocational-career education," should cause us to reflect on whether the common school should prepare children and youth deliberately for specific jobs. The answer for me is no. I believe that *all* students, not just the less academically oriented, should have experienced-based education through which the school draws on business, industry, the media, service organizations, and so on. And this experience should be used for more than an introduction to the world of work; it should be employed pedagogically as an alternative way to develop both content and skills. Dewey, for example, introduced woodworking in his laboratory school, not to prepare carpenters and cabinet makers but to expose young people to a different, less linguistic, approach to solving problems. Gardening is a vital way for students to encounter problems connected with the germination and nutrition of plants but is not to be undertaken in school specifically for the purpose of preparing future farmers.

As a result of and sometimes as a concomitant of such reality-based educating, students may make job and career choices and even combine paid work with their schooling. Some secondary schools even facilitate these arrangements. But for schools to substitute such ends for those of preparing the young for making wise choices in all realms of life, including work and careers, is to miseducate. Many schools do so and use as justification reducing high unemployment levels among minority youth, increasing apathetic students' interest in school, or reducing discipline problems in the school. These are not educational justifications. They constitute, rather, giving up on the potential of millions of young people.

Job training should be provided by the businesses and industries at entry-level positions (thus partially solving the problem of young people securing initial employment when they do not possess prior experience); by private agencies (for which student vouchers might be provided); or by the independent efforts of motivated persons who possess some general education and are willing to work with youth. Thinking along these lines gets us into fundamental issues of what schools are for and what education is. It also starts us thinking about the possibilities of an educative society in which schools are only one special institution among many engaged in a deliberate effort "to evoke knowledge, attitudes, values, skills, and sensibilities."

A second line of thinking pertains to the basic skills necessary to live in today's world. What is listed under Goal 1, "mastery of basic skills and fundamental processes," appears sharply limited. Either the subdivisions under this goal should be expanded to include most or all of the other 11 goals or else this first goal should be eliminated and subsumed under the others. The five subdivisions now included are lower-level skills compared, for example, to the skills under such categories as "intellectual development" or "interpersonal relations." They do not include any of the human qualities one requires to come to terms with life — sensibilities often thought of as part and parcel of the humanities. Norman Cousins puts it well:

> The humanities would be expendable only if human beings didn't have to make decisions that affect their lives and the lives of others; if the human past never existed or had nothing to tell us about the present; if thought processes were irrelevant to the achievement of purpose; if creativity was beyond the human mind and had nothing to do with the job of living; if human beings never had to cope with panic or pain, or if they never had to anticipate the connection between cause and effect; if all the mysteries of mind and nature were fully plumbed; and if no special demands arose from the accident of being born human instead of a hog or a hen.[22]

Goals 4 and 5, "enculturation" and "interpersonal relations," raise profound questions of meaning. How far dare schools go in examining the norms, values, standards, and traditions of the groups of which one is a member? Are the outcomes from such an examination to be determined in advance so that they simply become more information to be acquired? If so, we are once more dealing with training, not education. What do we do when students find shortcomings in their national heritage or indicate a preference for the heritage of others? Are we willing to consider the proposition that humankind is one?

It takes very little reflection to conclude that inquiry in school is very much constrained by taboos on subject matter; primitive thinking about our world and its people, among even much-schooled citizens; limiting conceptions of teaching as telling; and the depressing notion that our most cherished values are beyond the pale of analysis and revision. We say that our schools fail to educate; what we should be saying is that they have scarcely tried it yet.

Going through this list of goals leads one to the conclusion that schools are for thinking. But preliminary data from A Study of Schooling suggest that "listening to the teacher" predominated among students' activities even in the arts and physical education classes.[23] Other studies report teachers telling and questioning as the dominant pedagogical method and low-level cognition (information-getting) as characteristic even of discussion sessions. One wonders about our commitment to thinking in schools and whether we have any grasp of what thinking is. Again, Dewey reminds us of the nature of thinking:

> The essentials of thinking as the method of an educative experience ... are first that the pupil have a genuine situation of experience — that there be a continuous activity in which he is interested for its own sake; secondly, that a genuine problem develop within this situation as a stimulus to thought; third, that he possess the information and make the observations needed to deal with it; fourth, that suggested solutions occur to him which he shall be responsible for developing in an orderly way; fifth, that he have opportunity and occasion to test his ideas by application, to make their meaning clear and to discover for himself their validity.[24]

Goal 8, "creativity and aesthetic perception," raises in one's mind at least three different kinds of questions about schooling. First, do schools provide reasonable balance among the domains of human experience so that creativity might flourish and aesthetic perception might be cultivated? Second, since these sensibilities are so personal, do students have ready access to those domains to which their interests might readily carry them? Third, are the processes of schooling educative in that creative and aesthetic growth is supported in the students?

Aesthetic education and the arts, taken together, provide an interesting illustration of the lag between the ideal and the reality in our goals for schooling. Dewey came to see the arts as eminently illustrative of his concept of education as the reconstruction or reorganization of experience *(Art as Experience)*. Subsequently, statements of school goals at least referred to the arts — frequently under the somewhat suspect rubric of "worthy use of leisure" — but, until recently, the arts were regarded by very few people as central or basic. The term *aesthetic education* did not begin to show up in state goals for schooling until the early 1950s.

It would appear that the rhetorical commitment in goal statements has not been translated to any considerable degree into programs. Such documentation of classroom instruction as exists suggests a preponderance of teacher telling and questioning and of textbooks and workbooks. The common activities are not those one associates with aesthetic experiences. If one assumes that the arts and humanities offer unique avenues for creativity, then one is discouraged by their relative neglect. If one assumes that creativity is encouraged in science classes when students engage in what commonly is called "discovery learning," then one is depressed by the apparent paucity of such activity.

Preliminary data from A Study of Schooling tend not only to sharpen concern about our commitment to the arts but also to raise questions about the teaching of the arts in school. Although parents of children in the 13 elementary schools studied in depth expressed relatively low-level satisfaction with the arts programs, they did not support increased instructional time for them. According to the teachers' reports, the arts accounted for a small percentage of total instructional time. Consistently, students in all 38 schools — elementary, middle, and high — reported enjoying the arts most among all subjects and rated them the most interesting, but viewed them as the least important subject.[25]

On examining these and other related data, researcher Joyce Wright of our staff came away with the impression that the elementary school arts programs examined did not emphasize the kinds of artistic and aesthetic behaviors advocated by educators who specialize in the arts. Nonetheless, perhaps less emphasis on evaluation and more opportunity for physical involvement in arts activities, and the use of arts as reward or inducement raised this subject area somewhat above the others in attractiveness to students.

Schools, as our major educational institution, are to convert the array of interests expressed in the goals set for them into activities and processes that support the growth of individuals. To a considerable degree this understanding infuses the goals and rationales for them laid out in the preceding pages. Emphases in goal statements of the seventeenth, eighteenth, and nineteenth centuries stressed schooling for ends outside of education — for responsibility. Concern for the individual crept into statements by special commissions in the second decade of the twentieth century and into the sociopolitical state goals for schools several decades later. Clifford Bebell has provided an interesting catalogue of historical landmarks: "worthy use of leisure time," 1918; "an understanding and adequate evaluation of the self," 1927; "protects his health," 1938; "aesthetic development," 1953; and "deal constructively with psychological tension," 1966.[26]

In spite of this growing rhetorical commitment to the individual, we still are reluctant, apparently, to legitimate in practice what the free self requires for its full cultivation. Perhaps our sense of original sin is too great to permit much lighting of bonfires to celebrate the self.[27]

Even in colleges and universities, we don't want to talk much about what education is. There are endless discussions about course titles and descriptions, whether to divide the year into quarters or semesters, what sciences one must "take" in order to enter medical school, whether certain "weak" departments belong in academia, and how many hours of what one must have to graduate. But very little dialogue occurs among professors and students regarding what their own education and institutions are for.

Questions of school goals usually are settled in the socioeconomic-sociopolitical marketplace, not in schools. Functions get established by custom, by fiat, through legislative act, and by rule of the courts. They are perpetuated through the mechanisms created for the conduct of schooling. Education is both corrupted and advanced. The question of whether schools can get better — that is, be more educative — under many of our prevailing assumptions about education and schooling must be examined.

Chapter Four

On the Corruption and Cultivation
of Education

The goal of improving our schools may be chimeric. This is not to say that school improvement is impossible. But it is to suggest that, given the circumstances surrounding schooling today and what is needed to effect improvement, we — that is, our society — may not be up to it. Indeed, given certain of these circumstances and conditions, our schools may deteriorate and dissatisfaction and disaffection may increase.

I do not personally accept the proposition that school improvement is an impossible goal. But I do not believe that our schools will be better simply by wishing them to be so or by trying harder to do much of what is now being done. And my skepticism regarding many of our most popular beliefs about education and schooling, and the practices stemming from them, is such that I would predict poorer rather than better schools for the future. But this need not be a self-fulfilling prophecy.

The argument for or against my major proposition — namely, that our schools may not be able to get better — revolves around a set of related propositions. I present and discuss several of these on succeeding pages. My position regarding these subpropositions is developed just enough in each instance to suggest what I believe to be necessary for solid progress in education and schooling.

I remind the reader that my purpose throughout is less to convert others to my positions than it is to stimulate the dialogue necessary to the reconstruction of our educational system. What follows, then, are suggested elements for discussion and debate.

Proposition One: The norm by which the performance of schools is now judged is entirely inadequate from one perspective and, from another, corrupts the educative process.

Proposition Two: The affixing of accountability for improving performance according to the standard now used inhibits the creative processes required for significant progress.

Proposition Three: The virtual equating of education with schooling has so burdened the schools with responsibility that satisfactory performance, even if appropriate norms and standards of accountability were applied, would be exceedingly difficult to attain.

Proposition Four: The widely accepted assumption that since schooling is good, more is therefore better has resulted in an enlarged system which serves, as often as not, to deprive the educational process of the nourishing resources it needs.

Proposition Five: Although much of the support for our system of schooling has been derived from rhetorical principles exhorting individual opportunity, egalitarianism, and openness, in actuality the system is quite closed.

Proposition Six: The prevailing theories of change that use factories and assembly lines as models simply do not fit the realities of schooling. When attempts are made to apply such models in school reform, the results are usually failure and disappointment.

Proposition Seven: In spite of the self-congratulatory rhetoric to the contrary, education is still a relatively weak profession, badly divided within itself and not yet embodying the core of professional values and knowledge required to resist fads, special interest pressure groups, and — perhaps most serious of all — funding influences.

The implication of some of these propositions is that schools are not now in charge of their own destinies. Many of the changes and adaptations that school leaders should have initiated are now being forced upon them by court and legislative action. And, unfortunately, many people outside of schools who think they know what will lead to improvement and who are imposing changes on schools are not blessed with any special insight and wisdom as to what is required.

The Standard of Success

In Chapters Two and Three I described the expanding educational and social expectations for schools over a period of more than three hundred years. Beginning with narrowly academic and religious goals in the seventeenth century, vocational and social goals were added in the eighteenth and nineteenth centuries, and goals of personal or self-realization in the twentieth. These goals now encompass a wide range of knowledge, skills, and values and a kaleidoscopic array of scientific, humanistic, and aesthetic sources of human enlightenment. Nearly all of our children spend eight or nine years in the place to which primary responsibility for achieving these goals is deliberately ascribed. Most spend 12 or 13 years there; some spend 16 or 20 or more.

And yet we are content to use various combinations of the first six letters of the alphabet and two digits representing either total scores or percentile rankings as virtually the sole basis for judging the adequacy of an individual's or a school's performance. Large numbers of parents apparently suffer no pangs of conscience in withholding support and love or inflicting pain and humiliation purely on the basis of these letters and numbers. Similarly, others bestow gifts and lavish praise on their achieving children with little thought as to whether their marks were obtained with little effort, through cheating, or at the expense of peers.

But neither satisfied nor dissatisfied parents give much thought to whether their children's curricula were well-balanced, their interest and curiosity aroused, their talents unleashed, their creativity fostered, or their tastes refined. Presumably, the almighty letter grade and the SAT score tell it all.

Even when we are reminded that half of the students always will be below a statistical average and that we can never have most of the students above the 50th percentile, the next day we're back in that old groove again, hard at work trying to get everyone above the mean. Clearly, according to this criterion, our schools never will be any better.

My proposition, stated earlier, is that, from one perspective, the conventional means of assessing achievement are inadequate criteria of school success and, from another, corrupt the educative process. If we are to use student outcomes as a major measure of school and student performance — and I assume we will for a long time to come — then let us at least endeavor to appraise that performance on the basis of those goals for which our schools are responsible. This means developing and using tests related to the content and experiences that have been used to attain these goals — not tests often made of irrelevant items designed to elicit 50% success and 50% failure — tests pitting student against student but telling us little or nothing about students or their schools.

But we must go far beyond such measurement into what is,

surprisingly, a little explored terrain — namely, qualitative appraisals of what goes on in schools. It seems to me that how a student spends precious time in school and how he feels about what goes on there is of much greater significance than how he scores on a standardized achievement test. But I am not at all sure that the American people are ready to put a rather straight-forward criterion such as this ahead of the marks and scores we worship mindlessly in much the same way our ancestors worshiped the gods of thunder and fire. And so it will be difficult for schools to get better — and even more difficult for them to appear so.

Accountability

Use of norm-referenced standardized test scores as the standard for judging student, teacher, and school performance has led to a narrow and stultifying approach to accountability. There is nothing wrong with the idea of being accountable, but the problems and injustices in contemporary approaches to educational accountability stem from the fact that all the richness, shortcomings, successes, and failures of human effort are reduced to a few figures, much as one records profits and losses in a ledger book.

This is the familiar, linear, reductionist model that fits nicely when manufacturing paper cups and safety pins. During the past two decades it has been applied to the preparation of school administrators, teacher education, planning and budgeting processes, and, most recently, to the graduation of high school students. It has spawned a new education lexicon, with such terms as management by objectives, competency-based teacher education, planning-programing-budgeting systems (PPBS), and minimum competency tests. The expectations in using all of these is that education in the schools will improve as a consequence, with higher test scores serving as the ultimate criterion. There is no evidence to date that any such improvement has occurred. What school personnel need are not more standardized test scores but technical assistance in promoting effective learning.

The irony here is that the decline in test scores often is blamed on those "soft and tender" educational innovations of the 1960s. Yet there is growing suspicion that the much-touted reforms of the 1960s never occurred; they were, for the most part, non-events. In effect, we mostly talked about what education in

61

schools could and should be. But we did not actually carry out what we talked about in any broad-scale, sustained way.

On the other hand, there is evidence all around us that accountability by objectives, PPBS, competency-based teacher education, and the like have dominated the scene for some time. Is it not time to consider seriously the proposition that this cult of efficiency has failed to make our schools more efficient? Is the time not overdue for seriously considering other ways of accounting for what goes on in the education system and our schools?

How about these criteria, just for starters: How many students officially registered in high schools are absent today for reasons other than illness and are walking the streets of New York, Detroit, Atlanta, Denver, and Los Angeles? Why? How many high school and college suicides occurred worldwide last year as a direct consequence of grades or test scores? Why do some schools have trouble keeping students home even when ill because they are so anxious to come to school? Or what about this school administrator's criterion of a successful school: "I know this is a better school now because the kids don't throw up as often."

And how about the accounting implied in the following questions: What legislators have checked lately to determine how their legislation has affected school principals' paperwork, balance in the curriculum, parents' willingness to assist the school, or teachers' freedom to select methods and materials most suited to the needs and characteristics of their students? How recently, if ever, have the different kinds of specialists in state departments of education come together to determine what a secondary school would look like if all their currently independent proposals were actually implemented in a single curriculum? How many school districts have adjusted their inservice education programs and credits so as to provide time and rewards for local school faculties seeking to improve the quality of life in their workplaces? How many researchers are moving from those studies of a single variable in the learning process that yield no significant findings to those much more complex inquiries required for understanding and ultimately improving school and classroom environments? And how many teachers have thought at least twice and then decided to keep their mouths closed before saying that educational research is a waste of time?

These and other accounting questions serve not only to suggest the breadth of responsibility we all must share in seeking school improvement but also the folly of concentrating the bulk of our time, energy, and resources on those ubiquitous test scores. Perhaps the greatest irony of all is that even as we place a premium on high grades, we really don't know what they mean. My colleague, Robert Pace, pointed out some years ago that school grades predict school grades and not much else — not compassion, not good work habits, not vocational success, not social success, not happiness.

If misplaced emphasis were the only consequence of focusing narrowly on the accounting process, the subject would not warrant such impassioned attention. But what arouses one's emotions are the many negative side effects involving what is curtailed and what is driven out. My guess is that those relatively low-level cognitive processes most easily measured and most emphasized in the current back-to-basics movement will show some improvement in test scores during coming years. But my further guess is that more complex intellectual processes not easily measured will decline at even greater rate.

I am convinced that continuation along the impoverished curricular and pedagogical lines implied by "back-to-basics" will lead ultimately to educational bankruptcy in our schools and to an increase in youth alienation and dropping out of school. But, fortunately, the weakness of schools demonstrated in their rhetorical zigging and zagging is also their saving grace. Just as the zig is becoming excessive, we start to zag. Regrettably, we often are out of sync, zigging when we should be zagging and zagging when we should be zigging — but that is a tale for another day.

What we need now in schooling is to turn *from* the process of reductionism that takes complex human goals and processes and fragments them into measurable but relatively unimportant learning activities that are only remotely related to the important ideas with which we began. What we need to turn *toward* are approaches to learning rich in opportunities to derive varied meanings and to devise creative, individual approaches to understanding and problem solving. Robert Rosen states it well:

> . . . [F]or our highest activity, we do not argue that the end justifies the means; the means justify themselves. We need to extend this lesson to the whole of our experience; namely, that our happiness — in a real sense, the quality of our lives — lies in the doing and not in the done; in the doing is where our real goals lie. And these goals need require no rationalized ends to justify them.[1]

More is Better?

Propositions, Three, Four, and Five stated at the outset of this chapter, are so closely entwined that I shall group them for discussion purposes. Addressing all of the educational goals is a demanding assignment for the schools. There is great potential for internal conflict among school people seeking to achieve them. Many noneducators see successful development of the free self, for example, as sheer hedonism, interfering with the goal of responsible citizenship. Stephen Bailey speaks eloquently both of the school's responsibility to the free self and to the surrounding restraints:

> Surely, the educational system has no higher function than to help people to have creative engagements with the world of the free self . . . . If new purpose, new adventure, new excitement in living are to emerge for most people in their jobs and in their coping — if work is to be enhanced and coping is to be subject to increased mastery — it will happen in part because of spill-overs from an enriched world of the free self. But even these gains will be muted unless attempts are made to make the enveloping polity friendlier than it now is to the stages of individual development and to all conscious segments of the existential wheel.[2]

Interests that are only marginally or not at all educational intrude on the school's central purpose, as we have seen. Education is corrupted when the schools are expected to inculcate belief in certain values and traditions rather than promote open inquiry into them. Schools are caught up in society's conflicts when they try to educate for changing circumstances. For example, the pursuit of ecological studies often leads students to question prevailing economic goals. Such inquiry, an essential part of education, too often is curtailed.

Frequently, the schools are caught up in the pursuit of worthy social purposes in ways that seem almost to conspire against effective education. Desegregation already has been addressed as a case in point. School populations and professional personnel are shifted about to achieve desegregation, frequently making it more difficult for schools to achieve the stability they require for effective educational performance. But such factors are seldom taken into consideration when standardized test scores are being examined.

Many efforts to improve schools are frustrated by the addition of functions formerly performed by other institutions or not yet assumed through the creation of new ones. School programs lose their symmetry and balance. With no accompanying adjustments in the resources, time, and methods of operation to incorporate new functions, subsequent school performance is usually less than satisfying.

It should not surprise us that schools receive few accolades for what they do in many new areas of responsibility. The behavior problems not dealt with in the home are not dealt with satisfactorily in a school that now lacks what was once home-school collaboration. The more schools take on, the more vulnerable they are to attack and criticism. Further, the more they take on, the fewer resources they have for, and the less attention they give to, their educational function. Ironically, the more schools take on, the less other institutions assume any responsibility for education.

In effect, we have the grandest faith in and expectations for education, accompanied by myopic concentration on a single institution in seeking fulfillment of these expectations. The pressures for increasing the educative role of other agencies and institutions remain weak.

Although we almost always refer to school goals as educational goals and to the educational system as means for their attainment, what lies behind the rhetoric are goals only for schools and a system of schooling, not *educational* goals nor an *educational* system. The family is potentially our most powerful educative institution. Nonetheless, it is regarded primarily as a custodial institution wherein the acquisition or nonacquisition of knowledge, attitudes, values, skills, or sensibilities is an accident of birth and parents. Television occupies more time than schooling, but little sustained thought is given to its educational presence in the home or to its educational potential. The evaluation criteria are entertainment and the Nielsen ratings. And yet the family and television together, especially with the family as interpreter, provide a powerful educational setting.[3]

Meanwhile, our schooling-dominated educational system, like some stubbornly self-destructive dinosaur, seeks to adapt only by growing larger. It expands at the bottom by enlarging its feet; at the top by growing a longer neck; and sideways by expanding its girth. More is equated with good and still more with better. While the system is congratulating itself for effecting these expansions, almost everyone is complaining that the schools are declining in quality (the test scores are down) and costing more.

There are very few instances in our society of organizations increasing in size without increasing in complexity and becoming preoccupied with self-maintenance. Our educational system is held together by structural arrangements of such proportions that its maintenance consumes a large portion of the total resources allocated to it. One begins to wonder if the efforts to make the system better, according to the principles by which it presently operates, actually makes the education provided worse.

In expanding our expectations for schooling, we shall likely be disappointed unless we also broaden the criteria of evaluation. In expanding our definition of universal schooling, we increased the compulsory leaving age to 16 without providing appropriate educational alternatives for a broader range of clientele. Now, decades later, some people are proposing a reduction in this age to 14 because many young people find little in school to attract them and disrupt those who have learned to cope with the system. What an ironic self-fulfilling prophecy!

Similarly, we are taking more and more children of a younger age into the system and judging the success of this venture by how well these children perform on the conventional standards of achievement. We fail to ask what these children gave up in order to go to school earlier or how well the school is substituting for the parents who abdicate responsibility. Nonetheless, on the scoreboard we chalk up another victory for expanding universal education.

I am doubtful that we will see much change for the better reasonably soon, not so long as we simply try harder or operate our schools on the basis of prevailing principles. The dinosaur may collapse of its own weight, especially if more and more expectations and regulations for meeting these expectations are piled upon it. Legislation for sweeping voucher plans is now pending in California, with little thought given to the financial implications and regulatory procedures to accompany such plans. Unfortunately, such legislation is likely to appeal more to our pocketbooks than to our brains, and it involves only a short drive to the polls rather than any sustained thought and discussion regarding the past, present, and future of our common school.

Votes may express the will but not necessarily the highest collective intelligence of the voters. What we don't need now is more legislative initiative, particularly when the implications are as yet quite unclear. Some responsible legislators are becoming aware that their intentions, expressed in bill after bill — many of them underfinanced and most of them hopelessly tangled in regulations and procedures for accountability — have compounded the work of school personnel and increased the problems of the schools. It has been suggested by some members of the California legislature that they declare a two-year moratorium on legislation pertaining to schools. It would be ironic if any such moratorium were followed by more legislation that replaced one dinosaur with another.

Without fully realizing it, we may be at the end of an era with our schools. More and more people have become products of our educational system. Consequently, the traditional ability of the system to bestow advantages on those who partake of it is less clear; the value of education to the individual drops. Support for education and schooling tends to decline, revealing to us that underneath the rhetoric exhorting egalitarian and democratic virtues for education lie far more powerful, selfish motives. Many people, particularly those without children or with children already through secondary and higher education, turn their backs on the common school. Only the most and least favored segments of society fight for equality of educational opportunity; the former because they are confident in their elevated status and support schools out of a spirit of noblesse oblige; the latter because they see the schools as still the most direct avenue of access to social and economic equality.

All the rest want "the best," not equal education. Consequently, support for the common school declines and the desire for alternatives, often private ones, increases. The alternatives do not necessarily provide better education, but they do weaken the existing system. While challenging the uniformity and bureaucratic inflexibility of our system of schooling may be in order, the central question remains: What happens to the common school? Is there truth in the long-standing belief that our democracy depends on it? Or did we ever really believe what we have so often said?

There are two very significant signs of our being at the end of one era, even if the outlines of a new one are far from clear. First, assumptions about our schools previously unquestioned or questioned only by radicals have begun to come in for more serious popular questioning. For example, it is possible for me to question here the very concepts to which many of us have devoted our professional lives and not be regarded as particularly dangerous — indeed, many readers will identify readily with what I am writing.

Second, the less tenable long-established assumptions appear to be, the more intense the ceremonial rain dances performed by those who fear the personal consequences of new approaches. That is, threatened groups and individuals try harder to do what

67

gave satisfaction before, however inappropriate and outworn such behaviors may be. For example, it is clear that we should have established long ago firmer collaborative bonds between the schools and business and industry for the conduct of vocational education. The schools should not have shouldered this burden to the degree that they did. In so doing, they failed to produce the gratitude they expected from the private sector; today, business and industry complain more than ever about the failure of schools to teach the basics. As a consequence of the school/business-industry gap, new institutions and arrangements for bridging education and work are emerging. Many thoughtful leaders in the vocational education field recognize the need for them. However, some segments of the school-related vocational education community, still locked into old patterns, have been increasing the intensity of their rain dances. This is a sure sign that the times are changing.

The Problem of Change

⊁ Propositions Six and Seven bring us to the problem of effecting change. The model of change most commonly applied to educational improvement uses as the criteria for success those models of accountability referred to earlier. All call for precise delineation of goals to be accomplished, the use of goals to justify means, and measurement of the precisely defined goals. Applied to the improvement of schooling, the model usually assumes an institution incapable of improving itself, an institution not devoid of goals but with inadequately defined goals. The model also assumes more intelligence outside of schools than in them, and it assumes that a school staff is relatively impotent and passive.[4]

Among the many difficulties inherent in the application of this model, one of the most serious is that of motivating and capturing the energies of those in schools who must, in the final analysis, effect improvement. Scholars and innovators in research and development enterprises outside of schools rarely possess the necessary insight into what Seymour Sarason[5] and others have called the culture of the school. Furthermore, they rarely are willing to take the time to comprehend the viewpoints of teachers and administrators and to link new proposals with felt problems and needs. School personnel may nod in agreement with alternatives but blunt their thrust by transposing them so that the new blends compatibly with the old. When comfortable stability is threatened, traditional practices tend to persist, with reforms relegated largely to the periphery.

Also, teachers and administrators with seven or eight years of experience have been through several cycles of legislated or otherwise sanctioned "reform." While still trying to implement some earlier proposal, they learn that premature and hastily conducted evaluation reports "no significant achievement differences" and that some new solution is coming down the tubes. No wonder that the attitude of practicing educators becomes, somewhat warily and wearily, one of *déjà vu.*

One of the major ironies in all of this is that legislation is frequently enacted arrogantly; legislators assume not only that they know what is best for schools but that they will give it, even though school people may not have asked for it. Then, of course, the usual measurement baggage of accountability is attached to any monies granted. When no achievement gains result within a year or two, school personnel are castigated once again for their ineptness and the added costs of schooling. The politicians responsible for still another misguided reform effort somehow manage to wash their hands of such ill-fated enterprises; they are either out of office or are promoting the next panacea. Yes, accountability is a good concept, but it is as applicable to those who initiate change from the state house as it is to those who are mandated to carry out reforms in the classroom.

It would be easy to suggest that the improvement of schooling rests with educators, especially those educators working directly in the schools. But it would be dangerous and misleading. There is no doubt that educators throughout the schooling enterprise, aided by their colleagues in universities and research and development centers, carry the major responsibility for school improvement. But their utmost efforts would not be sufficient. The necessary reconstruction requires a collaborative effort throughout the whole of our society. How? As Margaret Mead is reported to have replied to such a question about change, "All at once."

There are signs of "metal fatigue" among outsiders who prepare concoctions for the betterment of schools. Their frustration leads them to turn over all responsibility — usually to the local school — with the exhortation, "There, I've given you the run of the kitchen. Now, you show me!" This reaction is as ill-advised as it is to take most of the authority out of the hands of educators.

Nonetheless, let us suppose for a moment that there were not the legislative and other restraints about which those of us in the educational profession have complained during recent years. The charge to us is to be responsible and accountable for instilling a sense of mission for schooling and for developing effective schools. Our combined efforts need to be focused on the individual school as the locus for change. That is where the students are. That is where their school experiences take place. Are we, individually and collectively, up to assuring that each school will be a healthy setting where education is pervasive and dominant?

We are a badly divided profession, each segment perceiving only a part of the whole and lacking awareness of and commitment to the collaborative functioning required for significant improvement. Too many superintendents see power as finite; they fear that delegating it to the principals will undermine their authority. Many are more preoccupied with budgets, crisis management, and public relations than with educational goals and programs. Relatively few have internalized, let alone articulated, the view that the prime measure of their success is the quality of life in the schools under their jurisdiction.

Far more threatened are those second- and third-level managers and supervisors who, not clear on their role to begin with, view increased autonomy and resources at the school site level as restricting and limiting their role even more. Their fears are not unjustified. I am convinced that education is improved to the degree that qualified personnel and instructional resources get close to students. I also believe that, beyond a few priority needs, adding highly paid personnel to the central office often makes education worse rather than better.

For principals, there is a certain stultifying protection in the ambiguity of their role. Being caught up in the demands of the district office and the routines of management, most of which could be done better and less expensively by someone else, many principals have no time for the development of programs and people within the school. This role ambiguity, together with the status elements of the job, causes principals to play their cards close to their chests and makes their lonely jobs even lonelier. Association with peers usually occurs through interscholastic athletics, thus tending to be competitive rather than collaborative. And yet principals long for collegial relationships with peers in settings where, perhaps with the help of a supportive colleague or university professor, they can explore openly the problems for which they were not prepared.

The departmental structure of high schools for both governance and program violates most of what we know about policy development, chops up the curriculum into fiefdoms that make significant change all but impossible and immobilizes the school in the face of pervasive problems, such as violence and institutional erosion, that cut across departmental lines. Teachers, in turn, are more tied to their disciplines and the teaching of content than oriented to the personal needs of children and youth, a situation reinforced by their professional associations and the prevailing system of accountability. The principals and teachers of elementary, junior high, and high schools rarely come together to examine the total educational programs for children and youth.

Teacher educators, for the most part, assume that teacher education begins and ends with the admission and graduation of students and has little or nothing to do with the school and classroom environments of teaching and learning and the role schools of education should play in their improvement. Too many researchers are preoccupied with research on single instructional variables that rarely account for more than five percent of the variance in student outcomes. Too few study the complex phenomena of schooling in its natural environment or develop the new methodologies needed to carry out such studies.

One could go on in this vein, citing also the precarious nature of a large, divided profession constructed on the flimsiest base of core knowledge and professional beliefs. But we have much to do together and little energy to waste on bemoaning the shortcomings of legislators, parents, and one another. We have met the enemy and he is us. What is challenging to me and, I hope, to you is that most of the paths we must walk are reasonably clear, blocked with debris at places perhaps, but visible nonetheless. And most of them are paths along which only you and I need walk to assure that a significant part of what is required to make our schools better can be accomplished.

Our schools can and should be better. But educators must take the lead to make them so. Large numbers of parents and students are ready to join us, I believe, in making our schools, one by one, better places to live and work. The slogans for improvement are, for the most part, meaningless rhetoric. Our schools must be reconstructed, one by one, by citizens and educators working together. Nothing less will suffice.

71

The Health of Schools

Most of this chapter has addressed the question of whether our schools can get better. My answer is that they are not likely to do so simply by exerting greater effort while employing current approaches to improvement and accountability. I concluded the preceding section with an appeal to educators and lay citizens to reconstruct our schools, one by one. To repeat, however, I do not believe this effort will be successful if conducted within the conceptual framework of the prevailing factory model of schooling.

The shortcomings of this model are so great that one pauses in wonderment over its continuing ability not just to survive but to flourish. It is difficult not to be awed by the apparent power of this ends-means linear model, in the hands of articulate spokespersons, to push aside other positions — not as alternative albeit lesser models of rationality but as egregiously naive examples of irrationality.

Three of these shortcomings impede the development of healthy schools. First, the goal-oriented factory model furthers the instrumental role of schools, taking attention almost entirely away from the *healthy* or *unhealthy* conditions in schools. Second, this model fails to reflect the basic realities of life in classrooms and, therefore, usually fails to predict or inaccurately predicts the impact of goals and means designed for increased output. Third, the indices of improvement used in the model are such that a school can appear to be getting more *healthful* while steadily becoming less *healthy*. I shall discuss each of the three shortcomings briefly.

On the Difference Between Health and Healthful

By *health*, I mean conditions of the school organism that allow it to perform its vital functions normally and properly. Health, then, is a present condition as well as a condition to be achieved and maintained. A healthy human being sets goals, makes plans, and gets on with the satisfying business of being. An unhealthy human being usually does little of this. There is a parallel between healthy persons and healthy schools.

To be *healthful*, on the other hand, is to be conducive to health; it is not health itself. Exercise is thought to be conducive to health, but a person exercising is not necessarily healthy. Indeed, if he is unhealthy, the exercise may kill him. Certain foods, rest, exercise, attitudes, and habits are regarded as instrumental to a healthy condition but we must be careful not to confuse the goals of getting food, rest, and exercise with the condition of being healthy. Harold Benjamin, in *The Sabertooth Curriculum,* effectively depicted the pitfalls of a society continuing to develop skills and abilities in its young that long ago had ceased to be relevant to individual or societal well-being. Good work on anachronistic behaviors predicts nothing about the health of anybody.

As discussed in Chapter Three, we often become so bemused with means to an assumed end that we make goals of them. These once-upon-a-time means that have become goals often are sanctioned by fashion or even by law. They, not the condition once desired, become the norm or standard to measure the condition, health.

Jogging is a case in point. Jogging, it is claimed, is conducive to health. Perhaps it is; not all the evidence is in. At any rate, jogging, various brands of clothing to jog in, and theories of how to jog are currently fashionable. In some offices, the story goes, nonjoggers have received anonymous notes to the effect that their abstinence is not good for morale. They even suggest that failing to jog is evidence of neglecting one's well-being and, consequently, the best interests of the organization. Jogging, presumably a means to health, has become the desired condition — and is put beyond comparison with other forms of exercise for the attainment of health. Those of us who do not jog can only hope that some jogging senator does not succeed in legislating *his* means to health as the required end, as has often been done in the areas of school improvement and accountability.

We can talk about healthy schools in much the same way we talk about healthy people. Schools are like living organisms, with characteristics that can be described in varying degrees as healthy or unhealthy. Schools, as cultures, must assume responsibility for their health and be held accountable. Likewise, the surrounding society must do everything possible to promote healthy school ecosystems and, like schools, be held accountable.

Achievement test scores are poor indicators of educational goal attainment, even though this is their prime use in popular practice. They can be useful when employed diagnostically to probe into the quality of education taking place in school and classroom. Almost any system of accountability that turns our attention to the substance and process of educating is more useful than one used to judge schooling only as instrumental to externally defined goals.

Corruption and Cultivation of Education

Accountability and Improvement

When schooling is seen only as instrumental to the attainment of external goals, a parallel conception of accountability is implied. But we saw in Chapter Three that education has to do with both ends and conditions, with the former tending to rise out of the latter rather than the other way around. (I use the word "condition" because the word "means" implies subordination to some external end and obscures the fact that educational activities exist, occur, and have meaning for those experiencing them without reference to ends.)

The prevailing model of accountability derives from a rational tradition of work and accomplishment that sets purposes first and then relates activities to them. In several states, this model has been translated into a series of steps presumed to be logical and scientific:

> The first step is to formulate some common statewide goals. Second, these are to be translated into specific objectives for local schools. Third, there is to be a determination of needed change efforts on the basis of some kind of student assessment in relation to objectives. Fourth, these needs are to be addressed through local efforts directed at the improvement of weaknesses presumed to be revealed through assessment. Fifth, local evaluation capability is to be developed so that some kind of continuing self-appraisal will be built into local improvement efforts. Sixth, feedback from all this to state authorities is then to be used in assisting the state department of education to fulfill its leadership roles, however it may perceive them[6]

The model as described — and I believe the steps represent fairly accurately the expectations for it — virtually calls out for attack on its assumed scientific premises. Most states set forth a dozen or so goals in the four major categories summarized in Chapter Three: academic (the three Rs), social and civic, vocational, and personal. The process of reductionism required to translate these into precise behavioral objectives defies the methods of both logic and scientific empiricism.

Not surprisingly, advocates and users of this model of accountability spend little time with the essential relationships. They turn, instead, to the technological problems of making behaviorally precise those otherwise rather vague statments of what teachers are assumed to be trying to do. In practice, then, the translation of state goals into behavioral objectives is not actually attempted. It is inferred, rather, that teachers already have effected that translation and need now only to be clearer on objectives. How accurately does this assumption reflect classroom realities?

I would argue that teaching and learning proceed in much more holistic terms. Hardly any learning occurs piecemeal, behavior by behavior. Only very low-level cognitive skills seem to be enhanced by highly structured, narrowly focused teaching. The more complex and, actually, more common learning processes appear not to be enhanced through precise delineation of behavioral objectives and step-by-step means to achieve them. Evidence is mounting to suggest that successful teachers orchestrate a whole array of factors in a complex system of interactions through which meanings and attitudes are derived.

Since the ultimate purpose, presumably, of this assumed scientific model is to improve an existing educational system largely by injecting more rigor into the specification of ends and selection of means, then one must ask how well it describes essential elements of that system and predicts the consequences of its use. Our growing insights into the nature of schools as cultures and classrooms as social systems increasingly suggest that the model does not fit the settings for which it is intended.

The processes toward accountability defined in terms of specific operational objectives and precise measurement of outcomes are pressures that many teachers dislike. Their distaste for this pressure is not due to professional laziness, recalcitrance, or stupidity, but is due to the uneasy feeling that as rational as a means/end concept of accountability appears to be, it doesn't quite fit the educational facts with which they live and work . . . The uneasiness is often — not always but often — justified. Some objectives one cannot articulate, some goals one does not achieve by the end of the academic year, some insights are not measurable, some ends are not known until after the fact, some models of educational practice violate some visions of the learner and the classroom.[7]

The usual antithesis to the precise behavioral objectives approach is the so-called "humanistic" approach to education and schooling. The "hard and tough" and the "soft and tender," approaches, to use William James's words,[8] have alternated as the desired emphases throughout the recent history of American education, with the competing rhetoric often becoming strident. But these are emphases to be blended, not placed in opposition, in the education of human beings.

Unfortunately, much of the debate between those in the hard and tough and those in the soft and tender camps focuses only on instrumentalities. It rarely gets down to the fundamental differences between education as science, dependent on scientific principles, and education as a normative process. There is little to argue about when the issue is whether schooling should be as humane as possible, whatever one believes education to be.

Corruption and Cultivation of Education

My concern is with the pervasiveness of the ends-means model described earlier and with our preoccupation with what can be easily defined and measured — even while giving lip service to humanistic considerations. This is as endemic to the professional education community as it is to state legislatures. Indeed, schools of education have employed this model almost exclusively in the preparation of teachers and school administrators and have contributed significantly to development of a supporting technology. I am not at all sure that the education profession, let alone state and federal policy makers, is prepared to support alternative models.

There is nothing wrong with the concept of goals and outcomes in education and schooling; schools dare not turn their backs on either. But for our schools to become better in significant ways, it is essential that school activities be viewed for their intrinsic value, quite apart from their linkage or lack of linkage to stated ends. An alternative theoretical perspective is required.

An Ecological Perspective

A useful theoretical model for viewing and improving educational conditions in schools is what, for want of a better term, I call an ecological perspective. "Ecology . . . is the study of systems at a level in which individuals or whole organisms may be considered elements of interaction, either among themselves or with a loosely organized environmental matrix."[9] An ecological model of schooling is concerned primarily, then, with interactions, relationships, and interdependencies within a defined environment. I use the term *ecological* in reference to schooling as it is used by environmentalists in referring to coastal mountains, open spaces, density of habitation, and the like.

An ecological approach to educational accountability does not eschew goals, just as an ecological approach to community development does not neglect goals. Rather, the criteria for evaluating goal attainment are broadened to include the impact that achieving one goal has on achieving another. Often, this results in elevating the unanticipated outcomes to the level of valued goals. For example, the absence of concern for wildlife in the residential development of a coastal slope is replaced by the goal of preserving or enhancing wildlife, even if it means reducing the number of residences. Attention is now focused not just on statistics pertaining to housing units but also to counting gains and losses in foxes, deer, and owls.

At the macro level, the metaphoric use of ecological concepts is obviously helpful in promoting our conceptual grasp of education as a system larger than, but including, schools. We come to see, for example, that the "good" accomplished by enrolling more and more 4-year-olds in schools must be weighed in relation to impact on the home. More parent energy is freed, perhaps, for other pursuits; but what is the impact on parents, children, and the family? The goal of getting more 4-year-olds in school must be evaluated on the basis of much more than a head count.

Applied to schools, the ecological model calls for descriptions, analyses of relationships, and the use of normative standards or criteria of goodness. Currently, the momentum for so-called naturalistic studies of schools is increasing rapidly; educational ethnography is about to become the "in" movement. But my guess is that the results of such studies will be employed largely in the ends-means rather than the ecological paradigm. By this I mean that ethnographic studies will be used to get a better handle on what appears to affect SAT and other test scores. This certainly is an improvement over what we do now, since it turns our attention more to the complexity of inferring causal relationships in schooling and perhaps reduces the tendency to seek simplistic solutions to increasing student achievement. But we are still left with all the educational limitations of evaluating and judging what goes on in schools in relation to a few easily measured ends.

The essential differences between the ecological model and the linear ends-means model lie in the way goals are used. In the latter, goals are only something to be achieved; they are viewed as "givens" lying outside the system, used to justify what goes on inside the system. In the ecological model, however, while it is recognized that goals have been set outside of the system for the system, these goals also are reckoned with as part of the system. They lie inside as well as outside. The ecological model also includes the notion that there are goals inside the system in addition to those ingested from the outside — students' goals, teachers' goals, principals' goals, etc. — and that these goals are not necessarily compatible.

Inquiries into the nature of schooling from an ecological perspective seek to gain insight into the functioning of the system and are as much concerned with the impact of external expectations on that system as with achievement of the stated goals. In effect, an ecological approach to accountability is as likely to raise moral questions about the goals themselves and the human cost of achieving them as it is to throw light on why the stated goals are being achieved at a high or low level.

Let me illustrate with my own early encounters with sets of goals that are internal rather than external to the classroom and the learning process. The school inspector, during my first year of teaching in a one-room, eight-grade school, commented favorably on my "activity" program (to my knowledge, I had not yet heard of William H. Kilpatrick), but he cautioned me to emphasize a strong math and reading program. If I did this, he said, I could do whatever I wished with the rest of the time. His words stayed with me. During the second year, in a larger school, I had an extraordinary piece of luck. It was necessary for the high school to take over a classroom in the elementary school where I taught, and this resulted in my classroom moving to temporary space in a church more than a mile away. As the only male teacher, I was chosen for this lonely assignment.

The children — all at that marvelous age of 9 and 10 — and I had a memorable time together. Except for the usual expectations for learning, we were free of all the controlling regularities of schooling — of specified times for lunch and recess, of classes and teachers next door, of the principal. We developed an unusual camaraderie. On dry days we played soccer, basketball, jacks, and a host of other games without thought as to which were boys' and which girls' games. On the many wet days, with nowhere else to be during noon recess but in our room in the church, we played checkers, did puzzles, and invented games while eating our lunches together. As a male teacher in a class of young children, I was something of a novelty. People watched in amusement while my brood and I walked the wooden sidewalk to and from school, the flock growing larger as we approached the school in the morning and smaller as children dropped off on reaching their homes in the afternoon.

One day I was chilled with the realization that cheating in the classroom and on homework was rampant. I chose to discuss the matter with the entire class, as well as with those individuals who seemed to be most deeply involved as givers or receivers of contraband goods in the form of answers to the exercises I assigned. Slowly and painfully, and with many tears, the picture unfolded. My expectations in reading and arithmetic, in particular, were high; the children wanted to please me. They simply joined in a benevolent conspiracy.

Our discussions led to a profound shift in the functioning of the classroom ecosystem. We talked about the importance of learning, education, and personal accomplishment. We worked out some reasonable and appropriate expectations of what we thought the goals for schools to be. Looking back, I realize that we developed a certain sense of ownership of these expectations. We came to the conclusion that helping each other with them was appropriate and was not cheating so long as none of us represented someone else's work as his or her own. And we recognized the importance of each person acquiring knowledge and skills. The goals the students earlier had seen only as mine were now ours.

It was of great importance to the health of the system that the children began to see the difference between pleasing me and enjoying me and in seeing how their enjoyment of me was mirrored in my enjoyment of them. We gave little or no thought to outcomes but a great deal of attention to each other, to how we wanted to use our time each day, whether it be with arithmetic, reading, science, social studies, physical activities, or the arts. I don't recall "disciplining" anyone, nor do I remember there being any fights.

Parents (who were invited frequently to visit and who sometimes came unannounced at the invitation of their children) spoke of happy children who wanted to go to school and who brought school home in various ways. In later years, I was told, teachers said they could identify the students from this group. They said it with respect and a certain puzzlement. And years later, as adults, some members of this class, still in the community, remembered our year together with nostalgic satisfaction. Largely because of a bit of luck, these young people and I managed to create a rather healthy ecosystem that was both pleasing to those within it and satisfying to the surrounding, sanctioning culture.

The issues of accountability are substantially more complex in the ecological than in the ends-means model of schooling and evaluation. We can no longer be content with standardized achievement test scores in a few subjects as the sole indicator of quality education. Indeed, we are now forced to look inside the system to determine how external expectations are internalized and affect individual and group life in school and classroom. What kinds of tensions are created and how are they resolved? How many children each morning become ill before leaving for school? How many take refuge in the streets each day?

We are forced to consider troublesome value questions. What constitutes a good habitat for teachers and students? What kind of support from the surrounding community is required to sustain this habitat? What are the signs of a healthy school and classroom ecology? What are the signs of disease and decay? What is a good school, and how do we know when we have one? Such a process ultimately would lead us to some basic concepts pertaining to *healthy* educational settings and activities and to some principles to guide us in achieving them.

All of us share responsibility for promoting the not-yet-fashionable idea of schools as healthy organisms as well as for developing and maintaining healthy schools. We need to make sure that state legislatures and school boards promulgate a full range of educational goals, from the academic to the personal, and that these are sufficiently broad to stimulate dialogue and alternative interpretations. We must strive to prevent legislation that assumes only one point of view regarding goals and goal attainment, such as an accountability system based on the reductionist model described earlier. Neither fiat, nor power, nor the rhetoric of scientism can endow debatable ideas with truth.

Let us hope that what is required for the advancement of education in schools will not present us, in the words of that venerable sage, Pogo, with "insurmountable opportunities."

Chapter Five

On Improving the Schools We Have

In the preceding chapter I addressed two major sets of problems regarding the improvement of schooling. The first pertained to a set of conditions surrounding the conduct of schooling, including divisiveness in the education profession, that will make it exceedingly difficult for schools to get (or appear) better. The second pertained to the conduct of schooling itself and the need for us to look directly at the conditions under which teachers and students are working and the quality of the experiences in the schooling process. I pointed out that achievement test scores are inadequate and often misleading indices of educational quality. I laid out for serious consideration the proposition that our schools may not be able to get better, given certain circumstances and principles within which they currently operate.

I qualified this proposition, however, by stating that it should not be regarded as a self-fulfilling prophecy. The circumstances and principles can be changed; a great deal can be done to improve our schools, especially by the people in them. Some of what can be done is discussed in this chapter.

I hope to reduce the paralysis stemming from the notion that nothing can be done about our schools until we remake the social order, but I recognize that some social orders are more conducive than others to education as defined in Chapter Three. I also wish to convey the idea that school personnel can do much to assure quality education for the children in their charge, even while government officials and others often are insensitive to the problems of the schools and frequently impose requirements that interfere with educating. And, finally, I hope the chapter contributes positively to the notion that improvement requires a collaborative effort, with less hand-wringing about imposed restraints, and less looking about for someone else to blame, at least before we have exerted maximum effort to fulfill our own personal responsibilities. What follows is directed primarily to educators and those responsible for the policies and regulations under which educators work.

A Focus For Improvement

In studying efforts of the past decade or two to improve schooling — that is, to improve output as measured by test scores — it soon becomes apparent that policy makers, educators, parents, and others have no basic agreements on where to focus their efforts. There are those who argue that school improvement is a waste of time until basic reforms are effected in the surrounding society. Others believe that state mandates or different organizational arrangements are required. Some think improvement requires charismatic leadership, better management, or both. Many believe that *everything* depends on the teacher. Others claim that student attitudes make the difference. Of course, each of these elements makes some difference; all of them and more, taken together, make a great deal of difference. It would appear that the proper answer to the problems of improvement is to move forward on all of these fronts. But this still leaves us with a need for focus.

Nonetheless, to get beyond our single, limited explanations and solutions would be a significant step forward. And, in putting forward only one of the above as *the* solution, it would be constructive if this were done without rancor and condemnation of other persons, institutions, or even society as a whole.

As I was putting the finishing touches on Chapter Four, a major newspaper published a letter to the editor by an obviously dedicated, experienced teacher who has given up teaching because the students "won't learn" any more. Responses to her letter are now coming in. The first is from a 1978 "graduate of the public school system" who says that if the teacher expects students to arrive late, cheat on tests, forget their supplies, and distract her at every opportunity, this is what she is going to get. The second asks, "How can a child respect his teacher . . . when all he hears from his parents . . . is comments about the terrible job teachers and the schools are doing?" This letter-writer goes on to say, "Many parents today do not have the capability, responsibility, or dedication to raise children," and states that parental inadequacies are reflected in their children's behavior at school. A third writer blames the sterility of the curriculum; a fourth sympathizes with the teacher who decided to resign, commenting on students' wholesale rejection of learning.

Meanwhile, in a different context and in another newspaper, I read that the problems of the schools stem primarily from running them as though they were businesses operated by administrators who view themselves as executives.

One cannot put forth much scientific evidence to support choosing one source of our schooling malaise or for selecting one focal point for improvement over any other. But, since most of the complaints are about "school," it would seem sensible to focus on the school as a total entity and not on some part of it or some factors outside of it. The school is where all of the elements identified come together, where they can be observed and treated with some all-encompassing perspective. It is neither so large as to inhibit getting started nor so remote as to be bureaucratically unresponsive. It includes more than the teacher but clearly contains elements that profoundly influence teachers' attitudes and performance. Also, it is the only unit of the total educational enterprise that deals directly, day after day, with its clients.

Further, there is evidence from A Study of Schooling referred to earlier, as well as from other sources, that parental and community interest in schooling fades rapidly when it is asked to address the broad issues of schooling as a whole. Parents rate their school higher and trust the decisions of local principals and teachers more when they are asked to deal with issues related to their individual school rather than with policy decisions made by some remote agency such as the state or federal government.

Agreement on the school as the place "where it all comes together" and the place to engage in a collaborative process of improvement does not require agreement on a common theory of schooling. But it does force greater attention to the school's present condition, the quality of life there, and some of the things likely to enhance that quality. Those who want achievement output may come to understand something of the complexity of achieving greater productivity. Those who are more concerned about the health, happiness, and safety of their children will find plenty of opportunities to work toward a more wholesome school environment.

Although I prefer to rest the case for the individual school as the unit for improvement on heuristic grounds, empirical data to support the case are increasing in quantity, quality, and variety.[1] Various strategies for school improvement based on the individual school and on the linking of schools in networks,[2] sometimes with accompanying research and evaluation, are currently being tried. Growing realization that studying the single school as an organism, culture, or social system — dynamic and thriving or apathetic and declining — has led to recent investigations into the characteristics of "successful" schools. The results of such investigations are not always clear or consistent, but there are a few common elements. The following are characteristics of schools that appear to be "making it."

A Degree of Autonomy. The school as a unit has a considerable degree of autonomy in the system or is itself the "total educational system" for a given population of students in the community setting. One immediately thinks of Evanston Township High School or New Trier High School, which are both schools and independent high school districts. The principal is more like a headmaster, in the British sense, than "middle management," suspended somewhere in space between the superintendent's office and the teachers. He or she does not have to fall back on rules and regulations whenever an important decision requiring independent judgment arises. Nor is one likely to hear the old bromide, "I only work here." A more common response might be, "The buck stops here."

That handful (5%) of the all-black schools that produced 21% of the later black Ph.D.s during one period of our history appears to fit the above description. Among them were McDonough 35 High School in New Orleans (California State Superintendent Wilson Riles graduated from it); Frederick Douglass High School in Baltimore; Dunbar High School in Washington, D.C.; and Booker T. Washington High School in Atlanta.[3] Similar autonomy appears to be characteristic of many schools that currently appear to be coming through the crisis of desegregation and effecting integration.[4]

A major principle that seems to operate here is that each school assumes responsibility for the quality of its own existence and is responsive to its immediate community. Schools must possess the authority and freedom essential to exercising that responsibility. Without these, it is difficult to see how we can expect school personnel to be accountable. We must reverse the trend of assigning most of the authority to remote levels of the educational system, obscuring the source of responsibility.

A Sense of Mission and Identity. The healthy school has a sense of mission, unity, identity, and wholeness that pervades every aspect of its functioning. What many schools achieve only in their interscholastic athletic programs is achieved for the school as a whole. Most of those connected with it have a sense of ownership, of belonging to a special place. And this family of supporters extends beyond staff and students to include, for example, businesspeople with no children in school. "I teach at . . . " or "I attend . . . " is spoken with a sense of pride.

Obviously, the attainment of such characteristics requires broad commitment to the concept of such a school. No single effort, event, or person is sufficient. There are specially planned homecoming days, a local press attentive to school activities and strengths in addition to the basketball team, the periodic return of school "heroes" (musicians, writers, and successful businessmen as well as athletes). One school has successfully increased interest in the total school by deliberately using the unflagging American interest in sports as a vehicle for "displaying" other elements of the school program at athletic functions. Another does it simply by calling for help whenever a crisis arises and then doing everything possible to involve everyone in celebrations of success. The degree of authority and responsibility invested in the local school appears to be a major factor in developing a widespread sense of identification with the school.

→ *The Principal.* The principal is central to development of a sense of mission, unity, and pride in the school. In recent studies of schools effecting integration with some success, almost invariably the principal was identified as strategic. In the successful all-black schools referred to earlier, again the significance of the principal — his or her values, dedication, and strength — come to the surface. Almost invariably in these schools, the principal is a person with a strong sense of personal worth and potency, who takes a position on issues, who is loyal to the system but not a pawn of the superintendent, and who is not cowed by strong individuals or groups within the community.

Usually, a good deal of dialogue occurs when problems arise. There appears to be a high level of agreement between the principal and the teachers regarding the policy decisions affecting the school, and the teachers play a significant decision-making role. Once a decision is made or a policy is set, there is considerable closing of ranks in support of that policy — even though there were differences before it was made. The operating principle is that once the policy is made, it is supported until the need for reexamination arises. Then there is lively dialogue once again, followed by adherence to the revised policy. Nothing upsets the stability of a school more than, for example, teachers who take advantage of every opportunity to express their displeasure over policy decisions they actively participated in making. The quality of school life depends heavily on a *loyal* minority.

Needless to say, some school principals are intimidated by the role sketched for them here and the leadership it suggests. They much prefer the protection of working within a framework of sharply defined and restricted authority. Perhaps President Harry Truman's oft-quoted admonition is relevant here, "If you can't stand the heat, get out of the kitchen." What is needed from those called to the principalship is a readiness and an ability for learning what the post entails. Unfortunately, they frequently are appointed for the wrong reasons and lack the preparation required. An intensive development program should be provided for them. And the superintendent, in particular, should be sensitive to the way in which increasing freedom and responsibility for principals is paced according to their readiness.

In recent conversations with school principals, I have been encouraged by their desire for a stronger leadership role and the accompanying preparation for it. Many chafe at the restraints under which they work, especially restraints resulting from state mandates that they have had little or no opportunity to influence. They express much less dissatisfaction with local regulations, because they either have played a role in their creation or feel they can exert influence in changing them if necessary. Many are frustrated, too, because of the amount of time they must spend on paperwork and supervision pertaining to specially funded programs that appear peripheral to their major responsibilities.

Interestingly, more and more principals are telling me that they and their schools would be better off without some of the specially funded projects and the demands that accompany these funds. They would be willing to settle for somewhat smaller budgets in order to have greater freedom to create comprehensive educational programs for the diverse array of students enrolled. This attitude of principals (admittedly from a small sample) represents a plea that should not go unheeded. When people appear to be carrying chains not of their own forging and are willing and able to perform more effectively if given greater freedom, then we should help them get rid of the chains to assume greater freedom and the responsibilities that go with it.

A Supportive Infrastructure. Healthy schools have a healthy surrounding infrastructure. The superintendent recognizes the school as the key unit for change and improvement, encourages principals to be captains of their ships, works directly with them as often as possible rather than building a wall of central office administrators between them and himself, and supports them even while disagreeing with them. A significant part of the budget — the discretionary part — is built from the bottom up, with each school principal presenting plans projected several years into the future, plans developed collaboratively at the school site level.

Such conditions are not easily achieved. Some superintendents are threatened by the degree of autonomy suggested for principals. Some simply cannot view the school system as a network of reasonably autonomous schools. For them, the uniqueness of each school must be blended into a larger cloth and must, somehow, become paler. Some superintendents in large districts see little possibility for relating directly with principals and fail to delegate the needed authority and responsibility to district superintendents. The already unclear domain of the principal becomes even more obscure.

Superintendents who do accept what is implied above often find that their own jobs become more manageable. There is no doubt in my mind that the school superintendency is one of the most difficult and underpaid jobs in our society. Top business executives function within a framework of greater stability and much higher remuneration; their positions often demand less loss of personal freedom. They must produce, of course — and much of their success comes from their ability to delegate authority and responsibility to subordinates. If a superintendent has some hope of living a life of relatively manageable demands, his best course of action is to delegate clear and considerable responsibility and authority to his most important subordinates: the principals of each of the 20, 70, 150, or 500 schools in the district.

The supportive infrastructure required for schools to become healthy, productive, and responsive extends beyond the immediate community and the superintendent's office. In a preceding paragraph, I referred to principals' frustration over the demands of monitoring and satisfying accountability requirements for special programs, conceived for social and educational purposes, that have increased the overall costs of schooling and elicited attacks on schools. Ironically, these programs are not always wanted by schools; they are part of the social role played by schools. The infrastructure, then, includes the state and federal legislative and executive agencies responsible for determining certain roles for schools and how those roles will be performed. The impact of what is enacted and required constitutes a relatively unstudied phenomenon seriously influencing the autonomy of the local school and its ability to provide quality educational experiences for the young people in its care.

Let me cite just one example of the way in which presumably well-intentioned but simplistic thought and action impede the ability of local schools to deliver educationally. A school district embracing both urban industrial elements and a growing suburbia has maintained for a decade a program of curricular and instructional improvement based primarily on certain concepts of pupil variability and mastery learning. The secondary schools, in particular, are organized into centers of curricular emphasis in which students proceed at different rates. Activities are organized around concepts, and progress is measured by a series of tests geared to these concepts. A centralized, computerized center is available to score the tests and provide specific information regarding performance within 24 hours. Print-outs are made available to students, teachers, and parents. They show errors and successes precisely, so as to give direction to the correction of weaknesses or possible next steps in the learning process.

There is an extraordinary fit between organization of the learning centers, the curriculum, and the many self-instructional and self-evaluative activities provided. Teacher-made materials abound. There is a little too much paper-and-pencil emphasis for my liking and too narrow a range in modes of instruction. But these problems are recognized, and plans are being made to correct them. The total conceptualization and its implementation throughout the schools, and freedom of principals and teachers to work out their own approaches and methods, are unique in American schooling.

Meanwhile, however, the statewide mandated approach to accountability, with accompanying proficiency tests, described in Chapter Four, is about to spring full-blown from the head of Zeus — or, more accurately, the state capitol. The frustration and anguish on the part of the school district's leaders are apparent. There is no way that the state department of education can improve on achievements that schools in this district have already made, with a highly supportive central office, over a period of 10 years. Do they abandon their own much more sophisticated system of diagnostic evaluation for something that obviously serves different, less educational purposes? Do they simply add it to what they are now doing, take time away from teaching, and compound the already heavy load of paperwork? To do the latter certainly will use up whatever discretionary time and energy currently are available for further refining and improving the program begun a decade ago.

The more one thinks about the insensitivity and, indeed, arrogance of those at the state capitol who have started this threatening train down the track, the more one finds oneself boiling up into a rage. This is not the way to improve our schools. We have tried it and tried it and tried it. And the schools get no better.

Considerable autonomy for the local school, a pervasive sense of mission, a principal who leads, and a supportive infrastructure will not in themselves assure quality learning experiences in the academic, social, vocational, and personal domains of the school's educational responsibilities. They do, however, suggest some necessary conditions generally neglected in society's efforts to improve schooling. And they certainly suggest the folly of employing simple panaceas designed to affect some small part of the instructional process. A school that is well along toward becoming a good place to work and study is the school that can take on virtually any project with reasonable expectations of success. Some readers will be thinking, "Of course, anyone can succeed in an ideal setting." But this is to miss my central point. Ideals are not given; they represent conditions to be achieved.

Instruction

It goes almost without saying that more than the above is required for quality education to occur in schools. But much of the rest is what happens in the classroom and is up to teachers. Again, the principal plays a key role in providing the support, encouragement, and resources required.

Basic to the principal's role in instructional improvement are at least two major kinds of understanding. First, the criterion of accountability for the principal is based on the development of a comprehensive educational program — one that does not shift from one emphasis to another, neglecting the arts when back-to-basics is the popular slogan or stressing responsible citizenship only in time of national crisis. Second, the principal purges from his or her mind those views of instruction that offer panaceas and simple solutions. We know now that no single innovation or intervention will consistently and unambiguously make a difference in student outcomes. Successful teachers orchestrate a dozen or more elements in their instruction in order to assure student success and satisfaction. These include ascertaining that students understand directions before embarking on the task, maintaining momentum, keeping students involved, using positive reinforcement and reasonable praise, varying instructional technique, alternating the length of learning episodes, providing regular and consistent feedback, and on and on. Teachers are more likely to engage in these arduous, demanding teaching techniques when what they do is known to and supported by the principal. Teaching, like administrative leadership, is a relatively lonely activity.

One must raise serious questions about the desirability of confining children and youth within schools and classrooms for approximately 1,000 hours each year for 13 years. Given the numbers of young people herded into cubicles ranging in size from about 900 to 1,200 square feet, the regimentation and the passivity imposed are such as to inhibit or even prevent educating. But since the purpose of this chapter is to discuss improvement of the schools we have, I shall stay with the conventions of groups confined to box-like classrooms. It is possible to improve considerably the quality of education even within these limitations. One only has to view the enormous class-to-class differences now existing to recognize the validity of this proposition.

There is no incompatibility between a classroom conducted with humane concern for students, using a variety of instructional modes with keen attention to students' self-concepts, and teachers' or parents' desire for excellence in learning. When students are involved in and excited about what they are doing (to the extent of being immune to distraction), excellent learning and accomplishment proceed. This involvement occurs, regardless of the techniques of external motivation employed, when the subject matter stirs the imagination or places demands on the coordination of mind and hand or puts the brain to work at finding new solutions.

How much of what is done in classrooms sets off such involvement is a matter for inquiry. My fear is that a large part of it stirs the senses very little. The subject matter of schooling is too much like meals on airplanes or in thousands of short-order food chains across the country. The problem is that too many people never learn the difference between what is and what could be. A meal is a meal is a meal; a school is a school is a school.

Nonetheless, some short-order restaurants produce a more attractive or tasteful meal than other restaurants in the same chain. And some classrooms, dealing with essentially the same subject matter as other classrooms, appear to be better, less boring, more productive places to be. The drastic revisions that probably should take place in the activities and subject matter of schooling carry us into concepts of schooling beyond those in practice today. They are not part of the school we have. Consequently, I shall forego proposals for more fundamental reform and deal with them at some other time.

The proposition I wish to put forward now — a reasonable one, I believe — is that it lies within the capability and is the responsibility of every teacher to develop a comprehensive grasp of those basic elements that comprise the process of instruction. These must become part of any teacher's basic repertoire and must be managed, so to speak, within his or her "span of control." As part of what schools do, teachers teach.

Referring back to the letter to the editor from a 1978 high school graduate, I quote: "In one high school class the complete agenda was: Read the chapter, define the assigned terms, and take the quiz." Her statement stuck with me, since while writing this book I have been visiting a good many schools. Some of them, at all levels, are being conducted in such a way as to renew one's faith in our public educational system. Some have depressed me for days after the visit. After I spent one day of visiting with a fellow educator, he sighed and spoke wearily, "I didn't see anybody teaching." His words brought to mind class after class reading textbooks or doing workbook exercises, with the teacher controlling behavior from the desk in the front of the room. This is shameful. Our tolerance of such behavior — and it is not as isolated as we sometimes pretend — is a blight on the educational profession. We are all culpable, but the principal has a special responsibility to assure that teachers engaging in slothful classroom behavior change their behavior or leave the profession. And unless teachers unions and associations assure that teachers teach, their future gains will be made with great difficulty.

Let me repeat my proposition, using different words: It is entirely reasonable to expect every teacher to develop and use a guiding framework of concepts, principles, and methods that appear to influence the learning process positively. Since our

91

knowledge of what is likely to be productive is increasing, it behooves every teacher to take responsibility for continued professional growth. And it should go without saying that the school district, as employer, has sufficient stake in this professional growth to provide staff development programs geared to the demands and needs of classroom teaching — not to the pet projects of administrators or school board members. Schooling is the largest (and most important) business in the country that does not provide for the continued growth of its personnel on "company" time and at "company" cost.

This is not a how-to-do-it book. Many good ones are available. It is a book designed to promote dialogue about what our schools are for and to encourage greater attention to and concern for what goes on in schools. Nonetheless, I believe it is essential at this point to sketch some of the elements to be included within each teacher's conceptual and operational span of control.

First, what are factors that affect learning? Can we get rid of the notion that somewhere "out there" is an idea or technique of such power that it will significantly simplify the tasks of teaching or assure learning? We know now that no method or other form of intervention consistently makes a difference in student performance.[5] To go to conferences or to take classes in the expectation of finding a panacea is likely to result in disappointment and will divert us from the larger messages awaiting open-minded inquirers. Even ideas of immediate practical value must be incorporated into a personalized instructional system.

Research to date suggests that the most productive instructional methods combine "interaction models" with "social systems" models.[6] The former include such elements as using positive reinforcement; assuring that the learning task is appropriate to the students (e.g., not hopelessly over their heads); redirecting the classroom activity when it clearly is going off the track instead of sticking grimly for the entire period to what has been planned; varying the length of episodes; being sure the task is understood; and so on. The latter models address the matter of sustaining a positive set of interactions among students and between students and the teacher. For example, the degree of involvement invited by the task can significantly reduce or even eliminate the need for the teacher to use controlling behaviors, especially abrasive ones. The teacher expresses positive interest in what the students are doing and in them as individuals.

It is particularly important that the teacher, in conveying

support and encouragement to the student, not be so warm and indulgent in praise that the student is given an exaggerated opinion of his accomplishments. It is imperative that students develop a realistic picture of how well they are doing. Teachers often stop short of providing adequate assistance in students' self-diagnosis and remediation.

It is important that a student's ability be defined in the teacher's mind not as a fixed capacity but as the capacity to understand instruction. For example, a child speaking Spanish in an English-speaking classroom has added difficulties unrelated to intelligence. Teachers must be sure that the students understand what the task requires. Good teachers often spend as much as 10 or 15 minutes at the outset of a class assuring that every child understands the instructions and is engaged in the task.

One of the challenges of teaching is determining the amount of time each student requires to accomplish a task under even the most optimal instructional conditions. One of the most severe problems in our schools is that students carry forward with them an accumulation of nonlearning, largely because they never had time to finish a sequence of work before being faced with new requirements. The answer is not the one frequently recommended — namely, the delineation and enforcement of arbitrary levels of achievement for passing to the next grade. The "passing" child may be only a shade better than the "failing" one; and our tests simply do not warrant such sharply discriminating decisions. And the learning deficiency of even the passing child usually goes undiagnosed and unremedied. A mastery approach to learning as recommended by Benjamin Bloom[7] within a nongraded structure offers much more promise for preventing the accumulation of learning deficiencies.

One of the problems, however, in programs geared to individual differences in learning rates is that the slower children become bored or discouraged when called upon to persevere for long periods of time. This problem can be significantly reduced if teachers employ a variety of approaches to the same concepts or skills; that is, the activities vary from dance, to field trips, to reading, to writing, to drawing, even though the body of knowledge or skills to be learned remains unchanged. Instruction appears to me to be too much oriented to covering material in textbooks and workbooks; it should attempt to teach fewer, more basic things through a variety of approaches involving all the senses.

Ironically, there is evidence to suggest that slow-learning children, many of whom would do better with hands-on activities, spend more time than other children in routine work and drills. It is imperative that instruction for all students, at all levels, be designed to employ all of the ways we learn — by hearing, seeing, moving, acting, tasting, smelling, constructing, touching.

While the evidence on positive reinforcement is not entirely clear, the evidence regarding negative reinforcement is very clear. A negative, abrasive pedagogical approach appears to corrupt the educational process.

The decade of the 1970s, I have maintained in previous chapters, was one of defining school learning narrowly. Sharply controlled approaches to instruction (for example, teaching for the attainment of specific proficiencies) seem to work when what is to be learned lends itself to this narrow refinement. But much educating is not of this sort. When richness of meaning is the essence of the educational activity, a narrow, controlled, or programmed approach to teaching may have negative rather than positive effects. No single pedagogical approach works for all kinds of learning, although much current rhetoric about requirements for accountability tend to mislead us into thinking precisely the opposite.

It is clear that some kinds of grouping practices, geared to appropriate instructional methods, assist learning. But no one form of grouping, used for all purposes, is successful. Students should group and regroup in various patterns for different purposes and activities, sometimes around interest, sometimes around comparable levels of attainment, sometimes around common learning problems. Efforts to establish homogeneous groups to work at different levels of common learnings rarely produce the homogeneity sought. More serious, however, is the fact that such efforts frequently lull teachers into thinking that they have conditions of homogeneity and need do little else to provide for individual differences. An organizational device is allowed to replace sensitive teaching. This is a major problem with the three reading groups traditionally employed in the primary grades. This form of grouping rarely provides for the individuality still present in the assumed homogeneous groups, and it often obscures the nature of the difficulties being experienced by the children. All too often it creates a self-fulfilling prophecy in determining success or lack of success in reading.

The foregoing summary only touches on teaching. Good

teachers orchestrate many factors,[8] no one of which makes a statistically significant difference, perhaps, but when taken together can make a substantial difference. For a host of reasons, too many to go into here, preservice teacher education is not geared closely enough to the instructional demands of the classroom.[9] But the shortcomings of teacher education do not justify excessive complaining and hand-wringing. We simply must assume that preservice teacher education is, at best, only a beginning and get on with the job of providing programs for upgrading instructional staffs already employed. To fail to recognize this fact and this need is to court disaster.

Leadership

One of the many charges against the schools is that their administrators, particularly superintendents, have been too little concerned about management. The field of educational administration responded. One definition of management (in *Webster's Third New International Dictionary*) is: "the executive function of planning, organizing, coordinating, directing, controlling, and supervising any industrial or business project or activity with responsibility for results." This definition and the concept of school superintendents and principals as managers fits neatly, of course, the prevailing, factory model of schooling discussed in Chapter Four. It may not fit very well, however, the leadership function involved in assuring that an individual school or a collection of schools will provide all students with educational programs designed to develop maximum individual student growth. Management may be part of leadership but management alone is no substitute for leadership.

Earlier in this chapter I referred to a newspaper article deploring the tendency of school administrators to view themselves as executives managing businesses. The writer, a high school teacher, deplored the management view of schools as stores in a supermarket chain. "Education is not a business," he wrote. There is a good deal to think about in that. I do not deny, of course, that administrators must have considerable management skill to handle finances, bond levies, and transportation systems.

The rhetoric surrounding the conduct of schooling in recent years has emphasized the need for efficiency. The message that school administrators must first and foremost be managers has come through loud and clear and has been heard — perhaps too well. Superintendents and principals have attended management workshops for school executives, often paying handsome fees for the privilege of hearing business consultants tell them how to conduct their jobs. A few years ago I was called upon to sit through a three-day workshop devoted to operationalizing "management by objectives." I was told that even my future innovations should be put within this framework and budgeted accordingly! What I went through was so far removed from the requirements of the research project for which the workshop was supposed to be relevant that the experience would have to be considered comic relief. The irony in this is that leaders in management theory already were questioning the mechanistic nature of many of the procedures school administrators were being told to absorb.

Having said all this, let me hasten to add that superintendents must be held accountable for a good many responsibilities best classified as "management." But the answer to most of them is: Delegate. Of course, the superintendent must know how to build a budget and how to read monthly and quarterly fiscal reports. Many know how to do this before becoming superintendents. So far as principals are concerned, the management tasks are not unduly demanding. Most principals do need help, however, in learning how to dispose of the routines they regard as management, routines that consume far too much of their time. Few know how to use secretaries effectively to free themselves for their central responsibilities.

The tragedy in the administrative domain of schooling is that we have moved so many of the wrong things to the center, thus displacing the right things and pushing them to the periphery. In many (perhaps most) university programs for the preparation of school administrators, courses pertaining to management are required; courses pertaining to curricular and instructional improvement often are optional. A group of associate superintendents for instruction and directors of curriculum (in a state that shall go unnamed) recently told me that it would be a mistake to list the exact title of their present positions in applying for the superintendency. The associate superintendents said that they would leave out the phrase "for instruction" and hope that prospective employers would assume the phrase "for business affairs."

I do not wish to create an unfortunate dichotomy between the concept of the school administrator as manager and the concept of him or her as educational leader for all aspects of the school.

My concern is that we too frequently sacrifice the latter for the former, with accompanying rhetoric of justification. In Saul Bellow's 1976 Nobel Prize acceptance address, one sentence in particular lifts the eyes and the mind from the page: "It is a long time since the knees were bent in piety."[10] In educational administration, it is a long time since we paid sufficient homage to the essence of our profession.

I believe we were much closer to this essence 30 or 40 years ago than we are today. Then, we seemed unembarrassed to speak of education as a noble calling. Interestingly, principals were viewed more as head teachers than as administrators and not at all as managers. The word simply was not used. The principals of the two elementary schools I attended (one of them quite large) taught most of the time, and the principal of the secondary school (medium-sized even by today's standards) taught several math classes each week. There were quite a few schools in the system before the first superintendent was appointed — and he was not called a superintendent. He was a kind of supervisory head teacher with a part-time secretary, and he was not very happy with having been "promoted" from his previous post as high school principal.

I realize that it was another era — so long and yet so brief a time ago — and that comparisons can be unfair and misleading. Nonetheless, there is a lesson here. Those charged with administrative responsibility for the schools kept learning and teaching at the center.

I realize, too, that today's administrators did not ask for a good many of the duties they are called upon to perform. And I realize what federal and state actions have imposed upon them, and how some school board members make demands that move the wrong things to the center, while at the same time demanding improved learning.

Nonetheless, for far too many school administrators learning and teaching no longer are at the core of their daily existence. Some of this is of their own doing. The words "school executive" have a nice ring to them. It is pleasant to rub shoulders and exchange jibes with business executives at the weekly luncheon of the local service clubs. "We must know what community leaders are saying, you know." And it is important to spend time with the representatives of IBM, Xerox, and Texas Instruments; there are important things to be learned about how improved technology can make us more efficient.

Also, crisis management, for all the hazards involved, has a certain titillating excitement to it for school administrators. A crisis a day keeps boredom away. Other people's crises become their daily agenda. With a crisis successfully resolved, one has done something tangible. We are becoming a rather hyped-up nation. Motion in itself can be a source of satisfaction.

But the improvement of curriculum and instruction calls for delayed gratification. The signs of progress are not easily detected. It is possible to spend weeks or months on matters of instructional improvement without the satisfaction of feeling that one has accomplished something. It is not difficult to convince oneself that crises, budgets, public relations, pupil transportation, purchasing, and the lunch program are what the top person is paid to manage. Leadership for program is the responsibility of the associate superintendent for curriculum and instruction or of the assistant principal. The wrong things are delegated. Yes, it is a long time since some of us paid homage to the essence of schooling.

Those of us who have been active in the field of education for three decades or more have lived through two eras of school administration. The nature of these two eras is faithfully reflected in university preparation programs for school administrators. In the first era, experienced superintendents and principals joined college of education faculties, usually on a part-time basis or during the summer, to meet the burgeoning demand for courses in educational administration. They taught rather practical matters pertaining to school organization, personnel policies, budgeting, and curriculum development. Charismatic leaders of a few school districts thought to have outstanding programs were in high demand for these purposes. In effect, they taught the accumulated wisdom of practical experience. As Gary Fenstermacher has said, "No one has yet outdone the common wisdom that emerges from simple experience, reflection, and informed intuition."[11]

But this approach has its limitations. One of its major weaknesses is that one person's experience often is of little use to someone else in another place at an other time.

The second era in the 1950s and 1960s saw the increased infusion of the behavioral sciences into most professional schools and their preparation programs. The behavioral sciences were coming of age, providing principles and generalizations of wide applicability that might help increasingly busy administrators cope with the demands, many of them new, of their rapidly expanding school districts. Social psychology, in particular, brought into focus essential considerations in serving simultaneously the needs of both individuals and institutions.[12] The leading schools of business administration were rapidly incorporating the new ideas and accompanying rhetoric, often changing their names to schools of *management* in the process. Could schools and colleges of education be far behind?

As so often is the case with movements in schooling, we quickly looked for specific, practical implications, not at the fundamental principles and concepts that might give us guidance. General principles always are more useful and, therefore, more practical over a longer period of time than hastily constructed how-to-do-it formulas. But, out of these exciting new stirrings in the behavioral sciences, we zeroed in on prescriptions that might help us run schools like factories or businesses. We became enamoured with input, output, and feedback loops; we made efficiency a cult.[13]

The tragedy was not that we attempted to become more efficient but that we erroneously applied superficial elements of the new scientism both to our roles as executives and to the conduct of administrative practice. We corrupted the educational process through overcultivation of schooling as a management system rather than a collection of loosely coordinated human systems called schools.

Now, as we reflect on all of this — and reflection is a luxury in which we indulge too little — we become increasingly aware of something missing. That something is what motivated most of us to become educators in the first place. The essence of education — teaching and learning — that should be at the center has been replaced for many by a whirling carnival of activity that is far from satisfying. As one of the best superintendents I know said to me recently, "I'm not an educator anymore. If this is the way I must continue, I shall retire early."

In seeking at the University of California, Los Angeles to reconstruct our preparation program for school administrators, we were advised by a group of able superintendents. Much the same point as the one in the preceding paragraph was made frequently. "We want to be educational leaders again; we want to make a difference in the education of the young." It is less a cry of the starving than of the malnourished. It is as though we stand in the land of plenty and yet derive little satisfaction, little nourishment from what we eat. Quoting Bellow again, "Out of the struggle at the center has come an immense painful longing for a broader, more flexible, fuller, more coherent, more

99

comprehensive account of what we human beings are, who we are, and what this life is for."[14] Perhaps those of us who are educators will begin to get some satisfying answers to the questions Bellow asks if we clear our heads of the smaller questions and get on to larger questions of what our schools are for and what our personal roles are in making them better places for people to work and to learn.

The emergence of a future third era in educational leadership depends heavily on the kinds of interests each of us places at the center and the choices we make in our use of time. If, in rechecking present perspectives, we are forced to conclude that collective bargaining, balancing the budget, and informing the public are our top priorities, then something has gone amiss. These are the conditions surrounding, complicating, and, perhaps, even endangering our jobs. We ignore them at our peril, and we would be well advised to make sure that they are well ordered. But to put these matters at the center, is to commit a fundamental error which, ultimately, will bring us down. *Our work, for which we always will be held accountable, is to develop, justify, maintain, and articulate sound, comprehensive educational programs for children and youth.* This is the central work for everyone in our system of schooling, from legislators and personnel in state departments of education to teachers and aides in classrooms.

The school superintendent or school principal is the educational leader presiding over one or more institutions and, as such, is responsible for all that goes on there. But he or she cannot personally manage the whole; delegation is essential. What he or she chooses to delegate is most revealing. In the first era of educational administration to which I referred, the superintendent was first and foremost, in everyone's eyes, the *educational* leader. To have delegated his or her responsibilities for curriculum and instruction would have been unthinkable.

In the second era of educational administration, superintendents more and more were trained in budget and personnel management; backgrounds in curriculum and instruction were assumed to have been acquired through experience. More and more, special preparation in the educational program became optional or was ignored. This ordering of priorities became the mode in the criteria used for employing superintendents and judging their effectiveness.

As the top educational leader, the superintendent must create discretionary time — time that goes to things other than those daily demands crowding the calendar and the clock. The way to do this is to delegate almost everything — budget, research, public relations, and, yes, even curriculum and instruction — to his or her administrative team. Only one member of this team should carry the "associate" title, and this is the person responsible for administering the instructional program, the person who will one day become superintendent. In so delegating, the superintendent does not get rid of the responsibility for the educational program. He merely rids himself of demanding details so as to have more time to think and plan and lead. The members of the administrative team carry the superintendent's authority and make decisions in his or her name. They administer within a set of values, policies, and understandings developed by the team under the superintendent's leadership.

Let us assume that the superintendent clears 15% or, happily, 30% of the working week as discretionary time. (Recently, a school principal in a large high school, with a complex, highly individualized program of instruction, told me that he spends only 30% of his time on managing the school; the remaining 70% is discretionary and is used almost exclusively for the instructional program. Most school principals with whom I have talked report precisely the reverse distribution.) What does a superintendent do with cleared, discretionary time? An educational perspective is required. The schooling of young people does not take place in the superintendent's office or in some nebulous territory between that office and schools. It takes place in individual schools.

The center of the educational enterprise is the individual school with its principals, teachers, and students. All of the rest of the district is superstructure, good for providing support, encouragement, and avenues of communication; but it is not where schooling and the education of the young take place. The superintendent who accepts this is a long way down the road toward the proper priorities and has taken significant steps toward making the job manageable and satisfying.

The superintendent must take responsibility for clearing up the ambiguity with respect to the authority of the principalship. The principal too often occupies ill-defined territory, somewhere between the district office and individual classes. In some places, the actions of superintendents and teachers conspire to keep the principal in this rather hapless situation of ambiguity. Each principal must be given the authority needed to develop the kind of school described earlier in this chapter. He or she must be given opportunities to acquire the necessary leadership skills. The superintendent's office exists to help — to provide resources, support, and encouragement and to unleash the talent residing in each school.

I come back to where I began this discourse on educational leadership. Recent years have been harrowing ones for school administrators. Too many have yielded to pressures and temptations to become primarily involved in fiscal and personnel management, public relations, collective bargaining, and aspects of the political process. Few are adequately trained or experienced in any of these, even though they must assume responsibility for them, and so it is easy to see why these demands have captured so much time and attention. What they must concentrate on most is education — its traditional and emerging goals and historical roots, alternative possibilities, curriculum, counseling, instruction.

In the pressures and problems of our complex times, too many of us have lost both our roots and our bearings as educators. "It is a long time since the knees were bent in piety." It is time to put the right things at the center again. And the right things have to do with assuring comprehensive, quality educational programs in each and every school.

Postscript

Improving the schools we have does not require new legislation, sweeping innovation, massive infusion of federal funds, tougher standards of teacher accountability and student advancement, or even an alternative theory of schooling. In fact, any of these but the last could be counter-productive. What would be useful, over and above the resources now available, is a carefully selected body of information on the functioning of our system of schooling and the present state of educational leadership, teaching, and learning in schools. Regarding the former kind of information, there is great need for the systematic gathering of data designed to show how decisions made remotely from our schools have an impact on the daily operation of schools and classrooms. In schools, we lack the base of knowledge required for comparing current school practices with alternatives or refinements and for determining the precise changes that might prove helpful.

Each local school needs to develop an agenda to use in comparing present programs with exemplary alternatives and to project the next steps. Is it reasonable to assume that schools currently do not have the needed data-base? Gathering such data could be a good place to begin the necessary collaboration of all elements suggested earlier. The resulting agenda could then be divided into improvements that can be effected quickly — that is, in weeks or months; those that will require a year or more; and those that will require several years of concerted effort. With a thoughtfully developed agenda focused on the educational program, collaboration within the profession and between school and community, and a supportive infrastructure, the schools we have will get better. All of the resources are available.

Elsewhere, I have developed the thesis that the individual school is in some ways a fragile unit, even though the key one, for change.[15] Improvements beyond the cosmetic are more likely to occur if several schools are joined in a network for purposes of sharing ideas, staff development, and mutual support. Ideas are more likely to increase in number and quality if these networks extend beyond the boundaries of school districts in order to assure variety among participating schools.

This chapter has addressed improvement of the schools we have. The reader should not infer, however, that what has been described will lead naturally to the educational system we ultimately *should* have. Such a system is much more than a linear extension of schooling.

The creation of an educative society may call for less schooling as we know it now, or more in some places and less in others. It will call for alternative theories of education and schooling, with much greater attention to educational media and technology and greater utilization for educational purposes of institutions other than schools. Chapter Six looks at some of the possibilities and especially at how to pose the question of what schools *should* be for.

103

Chapter Six

Toward the Educative Society

A few members of each generation are intrigued with the idea of utopia — an imaginary place, usually remote in time and place, with ideal laws, social conditions, and individual behavior. Although what is envisioned differs from generation to generation and from thinker to thinker, one characteristic is common: What the individual wants to do aligns compatibly with the prevailing tenets of the society. Utopian thinkers endeavor to portray those conditions that will simultaneously foster self-realization and societal well-being.

Education presumably plays a major role in assuring that the needs of individuals and society will not be at odds. In Skinnerian terms, the contingencies surrounding one's daily existence reinforce the behaviors thought necessary to the utopian condition. But, it often is argued, herein lies the problem of utopias, from Plato's on down. The individual too often must be shaped to the state's laws and traditions, rather than the other way around. Thus education is corrupted, becoming indoctrination or training.

Few utopian visions say much about schools. It is assumed, apparently, that education is pervasive and is a much greater responsibility than can be undertaken by any single institution. Utopias tend to make educating the young a personal duty, frequently to be put before rather than after earning a living.

Earlier, I discussed the dangers inherent in equating education and schooling. In countries such as ours, schools are called upon to solve almost every social problem, whether or not what is required to remedy the problem is educational in character. This has two kinds of detrimental effects. First, schools become burdened with noneducational functions and, in the process, forget what education is. Second, institutions and individuals not attached to schools neglect their educational responsibilities, largely because they assume that schools take care of all the necessary educating. These problems have reached such proportions in the United States that we must ask ourselves seriously what schools are for.

What Schools Should Be For

When we consider the long-term goal of an educative society — one in which the whole culture educates — one immediately thinks of a rural village where each adult assumes the obligation to assist in the upbringing of all children, not just those he or she has fathered or mothered. One drops whatever one is doing when a child asks for help, in order to assist that young person's quest for skills or understandings. Faulty upbringing is not charged to any one parent or teacher but to all inhabitants of the community.

If one were worried about such child-rearing practices as being mere indoctrination into the existing culture or too informal and unstructured to do the job, then one might create a new institution for "the deliberate, systematic, and sustained effort" thought to be needed. Would that institution be a school as we traditionally think of it? Are there some alternatives? Charles Rusch, who attempted to determine the kind of facilities and resources needed for the special functions schools are supposed to perform, created his school on a bus.[1] Los Angeles and its immediate environs became the place; libraries, museums, gymnasiums, flora and fauna, and a great many people became the resources. His role, as architect-turned-teacher, was to assure that this loosely structured process was not merely exposure or entertainment. It involved reading and talking and writing and thinking and, most of all, deriving meaning and reflecting on that meaning. He discovered that a complex, urban environment can be extraordinarily educative and that busy urbanites were ready and pleased to participate in educating the young without benefit of a place called school.

One of the questions arising out of Rusch's school-on-a-bus is how much those educating institutions not designated as schools might absorb and how much those citizens not employed as educators might take on. I am convinced that the answer is "a great deal." I am equally convinced that society, individuals, and the schools would benefit immensely if a vast expansion of total cultural responsibility for educating occurred.

But I am also convinced that this shared effort would not eliminate the need for schools. Those things requiring sustained, systematic attention would not be adequately attended to. The human and community resources used by Rusch would become saturated and pull back, arguing that their other functions were threatened. They would call on schools to do more. What we now have would be re-created.

What we need is an ecological balance between those potentially educative institutions that could do much more educating than they now do and an institution, the school, that carries an exclusively educational function. The line between education and training, between preparing for what is and preparing for what might be, would be less important for the non-school institutions. However, such a line would be critical for schools. Schools would concentrate solely on the "knowledge, attitudes, values, skills, and sensibilities" that require for their cultivation in the individual "deliberate, systematic, and sustained effort."

The proper role of schools, then, is to do the educating not done or not done easily elsewhere in the culture. In creating schools, one might well begin by seeking to discover what educating the culture already is doing well or conceivably could do well. In rethinking what existing schools should be doing now and in the future, one should seek to find out what they currently are doing that the rest of the culture is doing or could do better. To define or appraise the role of schools apart from the total ecology within which they function is myopic.

Few inquiries of the kind implied above have been conducted. There has been speculation, of course. Lacking the needed knowledge, I can only add to this speculation. My purpose here, as throughout this book, is to stimulate dialogue about what schools should be for and to inquire into what they actually do. As in Chapter Four, I put forward for debate a proposition and several interrelated subpropositions.

My central proposition is: *The school, as the institution charged exclusively with education, should take on only those social purposes that can be converted easily and naturally into educational goals and activities.* The schools should take on the cultivation of those individual sensibilities long extolled in humanistic thought and the aims of education (see Chapters Two and Three). These are the attributes of thought — understanding, relating, judging, integrating, reflecting, and the like — that require deliberate, systematic, and sustained attention. Beyond this educative function, schools should attend only to those administrative and managerial activities necessary to maintain and improve them. The prime yardstick for appraising a school, then, is the percentage of its time and resources it spends on what is truly educative.

The above proposition does not eliminate the necessity to provide in society other functions pertaining to the rearing of the young or to the enrichment of adult living. It simply is to define the unique and justificatory role of schools. Education and training might go on side by side (I deal with this later) in a community center, but the differing nature of the two functions must be recognized. Failure to make this necessary distinction has resulted in some of our schools being only marginally educative.

The several subpropositions are listed below and subsequently discussed.

Proposition One: If we suddenly were to find ourselves without schools, here in the U.S., our school-less culture would perform best those functions of the school's present role that many citizens regard as the school's primary responsibility.

Proposition Two: Schools currently perform least well those educational functions that the rest of our society also attends to poorly.

Proposition Three: The neglect or omission of what is most fundamentally educative is sufficiently widespread and pervasive to suggest the need for certain commonalities for all schools and all students.

Proposition Four: Those aspects of these commonalities that appear to have a significant training and vocational component should be part of education for all students and not just for those planning careers that do not require a college or professional education.

Proposition Five: Individual differences in learning rate and style should be recognized minimally through some variation in the commonalities required, and maximally through utilization of a variety of approaches to learning and through cultivation of individual talents.

The Basics in a School-less Culture

If we were suddenly to find ourselves without schools, the rest of society could be tuned up quite readily to take care of the basics narrowly defined as the three Rs. This is ironic, given the rhetoric and the pressure of the 1970s for schools to strip down to the fundamental skills of arithmetic, reading, and spelling. The video cassette home-learning unit, soon to be available for virtually any subject matter that can be readily programmed, is upon us. For homes not able to afford it, the provision of community learning centers already lies within the capability of several major corporations. Given the demand, these would spring up like supermarkets and be equally accessible. The money now spent on schools simply would be converted into vouchers to assure a reasonable degree of equity in the access to an education.

I hear, of course, rising out of these pages, a cacophony of protests reminding me of all the limitations of audiovisual devices, from teaching machines to computers. But the sound of arguments on the other side is equally convincing. There are very few instances of such hardware and software being used other than as extensions of teachers. Most studies conclude that teachers don't use instructional technology well; often, they leave it in a closet. But I'm not talking about whether teachers use it well or at all. I am talking about the creation of a situation where, there being no schools or teachers, something else would be needed. There would be strong incentives for using technology. And I am not convinced that the use of technology in homes and community centers for learning the lower literacies would be a step down from the widespread, stultifying use of drill and workbooks I have observed in primary classrooms.

Another response to these pages is that good teachers do not overuse drill and workbooks. They engage in the more creative process of involving children in learning activities of a more complex and compelling sort, within which fundamental skills are acquired in context and then strengthened individually as a result of teachers' attentive diagnoses. But now we are no longer talking about the basics, the lower literacies; we are into those higher literacies and sensibilities with which schools as educational institutions should be primarily concerned.

To belabor my point a bit, I am saying that we do not need schools today, in our kind of society, if their sole or even prime task is teaching the basics, defined as the three Rs. Such a function can be picked up readily and at lower cost with the available instructional technology and with a limited voucher system to sweeten the pot.

There would be no need for a large cadre of college-educated teachers to staff schools and classrooms. There would be, of course, a considerable demand for specialists in instructional materials, programmers, technicians, and the like. The need to take care of the custodial function formerly provided for by schools would have to be addressed. We might even want to use school buildings for such a function. But, again, we would not need professionally prepared teachers.

Soon, of course, it would become apparent that manipulating numbers and mastering the mechanics of reading would not challenge our young for long. The human being requires complexity. And so we would have to think about how the rest of "the day in custody" would be spent. Would we re-create the schools we have?

What Is Basic for Schools

The foregoing kind of analysis reveals rather starkly, for me at least, the educational bankruptcy of our schools when certain groups take literally and seriously the notion that their primary goal of schools is to teach the three Rs. Unwittingly, they announce their dispensability. A golf pro, dealing with something considerably less complex than education, would not consider his job done when the client had acquired a good grip, stance, and swing. Ahead lie the problems of hitting the ball and getting it into the cup.

Now let's look at schools from the standpoint of what society doesn't do well and would *not* pick up easily if, suddenly, there were no schools. Unfortunately, those educational goals not readily acquired in the outside-of-school culture are not at all assured within the school, either. As noted in an earlier chapter, success in school predicts success in school; and there is little promise that more schooling will develop those human sensibilities and sensitivities that education supposedly promotes. It must be remembered, however, that success in school conventionally is equated with high letter grades and achievement test scores. We will not measure success in any other way until we come to realize that successful education is that which promotes successful problem solving, sensitive human relations, self-understanding, and the integration of one's total life experience. Successful schooling is schooling that promotes such traits to the utmost. The evidence for this kind of success is found, first, in the quality of the educational experience and, ultimately, in the person.

The educational gap for the schools to fill has to do with contemplating, questioning, inquiring — activities that few employers pay for and that television allows little time for.

Indeed, many employers discourage both creativity and independent thought. A major corporation, in granting franchises, administers a test to aspirants. One multiple-choice question asks the applicant to check what he would do if confronted with a new problem, one for which he or she had not been specifically prepared: 1) nothing, 2) think up a possible solution, or 3) call the head office. The last is the "correct" answer. Few jobs encourage workers to evolve and seek new life goals. Education, properly conceived, is the countervailing force in complex societies that run, much of the time, according to fixed rules and prescriptions.

It becomes apparent that schools, to be educative, must possess the academic freedom necessary to deviate from many established ways. Their relative lack of this freedom is another major reason why schools indoctrinate and train more than they educate. That teachers seek this freedom is evident from our Study of Schooling, referred to earlier, where teachers at all levels claimed that they depend relatively little on state and local curriculum guides for what and how they teach. Their chief guide is their own experience and professional training.[2]

If this be so, then one hope — short of a complete overhaul of the whole of society — for the schools to become educative is for some teachers, at least, to have the best possible general and professional education. According to Joseph W. Gauld, "Over the last 30 years, their level of professionalism — never very high to begin with — has practically been reduced to the level of a file clerk."[3] I tend to agree. Partly as a consequence, the public does not regard teachers as professionals and, too often, the teacher's self-concept is not as a professional, either. "The system," says Gauld, "failed to develop in them a professional sensitivity . . . so they, themselves, have no real confidence in the depth of their effectiveness."[4]

I am inclined to agree with Lawrence Cremin that teachers should be prepared at the level of a professional doctorate. There are no doctors who hold only A.B. or M.A. degrees; there are only doctors who hold the M.D. No more should the word "teacher" cover so many levels of preparation and thus obscure what professional preparation is or should be. Ironically, few who secure the doctorate teach; they administer, or manage, or run the transportation system. Education is the only profession I know that consistently places its most highly prepared personnel farthest from the activities that are at its heart and for which the entire profession is held accountable. Studies of aides in classrooms have not demonstrated that the teachers they assist spend more of their time on teaching or otherwise guiding children's learning than do teachers without aides.

I am saying, then, that promotion of the higher literacies — those educational matters not well attended to in a school-less society — requires persons as teachers who not only are themselves proficient in these literacies but who also know how to teach them. This means general and professional education extending substantially beyond what all but a few teachers secure today. I object, however, to the possibly inferred implication that teachers need only more of what is now taught in colleges and graduate schools. A very large part of undergraduate education today is in no way general education. Much of it is vocational training or highly specialized professional preparation. Much of the chemistry, mathematics, literature, and history taught is designed for those relatively few in the classes who will become specialists or professionals in these fields, not for the many who need to understand more about our civilization. In the same vein, I am not at all sure that there are a dozen schools of education in the country providing at any degree level the breadth and depth of preparation required for teachers who are to be professionals and not merely technicians. Now that we have a surplus of teachers, the time is right to elevate teacher preparation to several years of graduate work — at least to the level of the degree, "candidate in education," approximately two years beyond the master's degree.

I do not wish to imply, either, that every primary classroom will be staffed with a Ph.D. or Ed.D. But let us imagine an elementary school, for example, staffed by 18 adults, nine of whom are prepared at the level of most of today's teachers, five are apprentices, and four are fully prepared professionals — one with a thorough understanding of human growth and learning, one with keen insight into language acquisition, one with special competence in mathematics education, and one with expertise in the diagnosis and remediation of reading disabilities — all teaching and all planning together in company with a professional principal, specially prepared in curriculum development and with leadership ability. Such a school would be a better and probably much less costly place than a school cluttered and fragmented with specialized programs designed to compensate for the fact that most schools are marginally educative in the first place. More of what is not education does not make for better schools.

111

Toward the Educative Society

If we set as goals for schools all those complexities and imponderables of educating we have tried to define for centuries (and never quite succeeded), we will both challenge bright and creative people to prepare for teaching and elevate the field as a profession. For years, we have been heading in precisely the opposite direction, trivializing what education is and asking only that practitioners be technicians. Fortunately, we have managed to attract a good many people who want and are capable of much more. If we demanded that our schools be educative, in the true sense of that word, and little else, it is just possible that we could develop a profession capable of resisting the simplistic folly thrust upon and too readily accepted by our schools in recent years. Such, it seems to me, is an essential, if not sufficient, ingredient of the schools we need.

Commonalities for Society's Schools

If the development of a compassionate understanding of humankind, the ability to solve unfamiliar problems, the ability to establish appropriate relationships, and the ability to achieve personal goals are casually or inadequately attended to in our society, then educational institutions are needed to take up the slack. But society can ill afford to create such institutions and leave them, in turn, to be casual or indifferent about their educational responsibilities. It is far too late in this book to address anew the issues of accountability involved in assuring the proper checks and balances. My positions and my general answers are scattered throughout the preceding chapters. The matter before us now is the school's responsibility for the education gap.

The core of my argument is that most of what is done by the common school should be common for all its students. What a surprising remark from a man who has devoted much of his professional career to the cause of human uniqueness and individuality! But I never have argued for differing paths, or for free choice of subject matter for students in our schools. Indeed, I am fearful of any kind of tracking or unguided self-selection that could set in motion a self-fulfilling prophecy, separating losers from winners. Much of what has been done in the name of individualization has resulted, unwittingly perhaps, in depriving children and youth of experiences they should have and in limiting their aspirations. Getting "D" in a subject, if we must continue with such distinctions, may be a much lesser indignity

112

than assignment to a class not yet imbued with status and possessing negligible educational value. If there is something important that society does not commonly do, and if this is what schools exist to do, then schools had better commonly do it.

Where individualization should be fostered is in what students get out of what is commonly encountered. We corrupt the educational process, not by having all students grapple with the nature of revolutions, but by seeking a common set of outcomes and conclusions regarding the French, Russian, or American revolutions. The miseducative process begins early and is pervasive in schooling. The teacher in a primary classroom asks a question warranting several interpretations but has a preferred one in mind. The children join in a guessing game until one of them gets the "right" answer — the one the teacher has in mind — and is verbally rewarded. The children quickly learn the teacher's signs of approval and parrot the approved answer. These children have no learning experience, let alone a common one. The correct guessers are inappropriately rewarded but become school-wise and are usually successful. But education is not assured for either the rewarded guessers or those who learn to parrot dimly perceived answers to dimly understood questions. What I am describing is all too common at all levels of schooling.

What I am *not* proposing as commonalities is a set of detached bodies of subject matter to be "covered" by all. But surely it is possible to identify areas of human endeavor and expression that promise rich and varied individual encounters with concepts and ideas of potentially powerful meaning. Marshall Gordon effectively makes the distinction I am struggling for, essentially a distinction between knowledge as something external to oneself and knowledge as personal experience and meaning:

> It is my contention that although mathematics is commonly viewed and presented as a deductively determined body of knowledge, it is nevertheless fundamentally a personal experience; the 'terror and triumph' of constructing mathematical knowledge clearly signals its subjective dimension. In my estimation, this conflict — both personal and epistemological — derives from a failure to acknowledge the personal acts of choosing and valuing in our finely polished, impersonal mathematics curriculum — . . . .[5]

Vocational as General Education

In recent years, various reformers have again proposed tracking — the division of students into differentiated curricula on the basis of aptitude or achievement — as the solution to the diversity of population in our schools. What they seem to be unaware of is that many of our schools — particularly high schools — already are tracked. Of the 13 high schools in our Study of Schooling, eight were tracked in all four of the major academic areas: English, mathematics, science, and social studies. The other five high schools tracked students in three of these subject areas.[6]

The evidence as to whether students achieve better under such circumstances is, in general, mixed for the students in the advanced or superior tracks; generally negative for those in the slower tracks. But such data do not address the major issue, which is one of equity. To what degree are some students deprived of the richest opportunities for personal growth and identification with their civilization when they are placed in a slow track?

The issue is sharpened when one examines student assignment and selection practices in academic and vocational programs. A large proportion of students having difficulty (i.e., getting low marks) are counseled into vocational programs. This will be denied by many principals, counselors, and vocational education teachers who point to the number of college-bound students in vocational education classes. But, almost always, college-bound students take vocational courses as electives and do not jeopardize their college entrance requirements. Some schools point proudly to the number of students who go directly to skilled and semi-skilled jobs from their high school vocational education classes. However, there is evidence that this transition is more the exception than the rule.[7] An occasional high school boasts experience-based programs that appear to offer a nice balance of the academic and the vocational, but these usually reach only a small percentage of the student body.

The point I wish to make is that most of those practices serving to differentiate academic students from students who must settle for something less (and the "less" is clearly understood, if not always clearly articulated, by all involved) discriminate against both groups. Both miss something not likely to be readily available elsewhere in society and for which, presumably, they attended school. One group is likely to begin struggling for a living with little understanding of or time and inclination for all of the rich, individual experiences to be derived from the arts and humanities. The other is likely to be ill-equipped to deal satisfactorily and satisfyingly with the demands of the technology encountered in one's daily existence. I am convinced

114

that a basic understanding of electricity, gasoline and diesel engines, and computers, together with a modicum of eye-hand coordination, are essential to modern living — and I speak feelingly from the depths of illiteracy and incompetence in such matters.

Individual Differences

One of the most intriguing characteristics of humankind is that a single species can vary so from individual to individual — in interests, ways of thinking, color, ways of responding to sound or scent. One of the most remarkable things about education is that it expands what can be commonly shared by all this human diversity and at the same time differentiates one person from another. For me, the most interesting family or class is the one that has most in common (e.g., grandparents and grandchildren able to engage together in dialogue about politics or music) and the widest range of individual pursuits (e.g. each individual is developing what Whitehead called style in some talent).

Elsewhere, I have sketched what I consider to be some of the essential ingredients for successive phases of schooling.[8] I shall not repeat the list here. But three of these ingredients bear rather directly on the issue of what I see as a necessary balance of commonality and uniqueness in the essentially personal experience that is education. One of these I already have touched upon. It has to do with promoting maximum individuality in the personal experience of that which is being commonly encountered. If the good teacher has a goal in mind, it is not that a precise objective shall be attained but that individual meaning will be derived.

It is my view that much individualization in learning has gone in precisely the wrong direction. Most efforts at individualization have been devoted to devising individual stimuli that are likely to promote identical learning. As a consequence, some of the best-known projects in individualized instruction have provided little more than programmed courses through which students proceeded individually, using do-it-yourself tests from a kit and completing them at their own rates of speed. Actually, the notion of differentiated stimuli is a myth; rather, the same stimuli are encountered but at different times. Group discussion, if it occurs at all, usually arises out of some common difficulty noted by a teacher.

In my judgment, this is the reverse of how to proceed in most learnings. A group provides the ideal testing ground for checking

115

out personal meaning, gaining new insights, and clarifying thoughts. Discussion is enhanced by group diversity; homogeneity in interest, background, and ability is a liability. The Great Books seminars provide a model at the adult level. Participants read a book in common, deriving initial meanings individually. The stimulating next stage is the exchange of those meanings in a diverse group representing a wide range of schooling, interests, careers, and the like. In elementary and secondary school classrooms, exercises designed to address deficiencies in the mechanics of reading, spelling, or mathematics would follow group discussion. And such remediation would be highly individualized.

A second aspect of individuality relates to the school's responsibility for some commonality in learning. We give up too soon on general education in a process of separating academic from nonacademic students; therefore, I believe we should try to deal better with fewer topics for more students. I am not suggesting that there are certain topics I wish students everywhere to deal with commonly. Rather, the topics should rise out of the context of the students' encounters with their universe. What students should grapple with in common are the concepts of time, space, number, form, line, and conservation underlying interchangeable sets of topics and the processes of personally identifying with these concepts. During the curriculum reform movement of the 1960s, we referred to these as the structure of knowledge and ways of knowing, respectively.

Students should not be taught *a* way of knowing. They should have encounters with many ways through many different kinds of media, and they should develop a repertoire of approaches. Instead, we have converted our young into answer-getters. We often state that children and youth should learn how to learn, but relatively little of what goes on in school is directed to such an end.

I would argue, then, for teaching just a very few basic concepts through every possible means. Not just by reading and writing, but by dancing, drawing, constructing, touching, thinking, talking, shaping, planning; and not just one of these ways for each separate concept, but all of these ways for each concept. In this way schools not only encourage versatility but, in addition, give the greatest possible assurance that each student will learn because of the variety of learning modes that are brought into play. However, schools must guide each student beyond personally comfortable ways of learning into all those

116

alternatives lying just beyond the comfort zone.

A third provision for individuality in schools within the commonality of learnings is the development of individual talent. It is my belief that each child or youth, over three or four years, should develop, to a level of considerable mastery, some talent in mathematics, the arts, athletics, handicrafts, or whatever. So much the better if, after he masters one area, another is added during each successive phase of schooling. It is reasonable to conceive, then, of young adults with two or three individual interests now at a level of development that is likely to provide deep, personal satisfaction throughout the whole of life.

Ironically, in spite of all the rhetoric about individuality, most school activities designed for recreation and lifelong enjoyment cannot be enjoyed later. For example, I played baseball, basketball, and soccer in school, but enjoyment of these later would require recruiting eight, four, or 10 others. In our sample of junior high schools in our Study of Schooling, most physical education activities were found to be group-oriented. Even in individual sports the emphasis was on competition rather than the refinement of personal skills.[9]

While the advantages of embarking early on pursuits likely to provide deep, personal satisfaction should be self-evident, there is another important point to consider. I believe there are two important kinds of transfer value in developing a talent and the accompanying awareness of the ingredients of that talent. First, freedom to use a portion of one's time on what is personally and deeply satisfying helps one through those other demands of life that are necessary but offer little satisfaction. Second, there is, I think, a deeper appreciation of what goes into any area of expertise and a greater readiness to look for those elements that comprise proficiency in some other field. One may be able to develop style in only a very few things, but life is enriched with the development of connoisseurship in more than a few.

We lament the fare provided by television and deplore the devotion of so many to what so often is momentarily titillating and ultimately stultifying. Yet persons with rich personal resources, living full lives, actually have difficulty scheduling time for television and usually do so only after careful study of projected offerings. Such persons almost invariably are the ones who have cultivated pursuits requiring active intellectual or physical involvement and who have the ability to make discriminating judgments within a large domain of personal accomplishments.

Alternative Scenarios for Schooling and Education

In preceding chapters I have argued that the school is only part of what educates in our society and that it must not be equated with the whole of education. I have said that schools are only in part — frequently only in small part — educational institutions. And I have argued that the direction for reconstruction is toward having our schools be maximally educational and minimally everything else. Even given substantial progress in such a direction, however, our schools will not provide all the educating humankind requires.

Such reconstruction raises interesting possibilities for alternatives in the educational ecology. Some important things pushed out of schools would be absorbed elsewhere. Some heretofore non-educational institutions would become more educative. New educational settings would emerge. However, there is a chance that scenarios quite different from what I would prefer will be played out. Let us examine some of these scenarios.

Scenario One. A quick reading of the signs, *circa* 1980, suggests a continuance into this decade of these excesses of the 1970s: reductionism with respect to educational goals and practices, preoccupation with minimum competencies, excessive testing, and measured outcomes as the sole criteria of school and student performance.

Implementation of a narrow interpretation of back-to-basics soon will raise questions about the length of the school day and, perhaps, will bring proposals for cutting costs by shortening it, with accompanying elimination of "non-basics." However, the country's economic condition is a deterrent to either absorbing the young into the work force or creating youth corps or other kinds of institutions to use up non-school time.

A more careful reading of the signs might suggest, however, that the movement referred to above peaked in the mid to late 1970s. The momentum of the movement continues to affect practices, with states copying other states; but the questioning has set in. Indeed, there are signs that another humanistic cycle of reform is brewing.

The great uncertainty is whether the countervailing forces will focus on the public school system or will concentrate on alternatives to it. Many humanistically oriented reformers have given up on the schools and are thoroughly disenchanted with and exhausted from the efforts of the 1960s. Many do not want a voucher system, since they see it as only another way of perpetuating schools preoccupied with the wrong things. Ironically, these are essentially the same arguments employed by advocates of the voucher plan.

As I said in Chapter Four, I do not believe it is possible for our schools to get better under the prevailing emphasis on performance and accountability. Consequently, if schools go on into the twenty-first century and do nothing more than refine in practice the rhetoric of the 1970s, then we can expect to see the general dismantling of the public school system as we now know it.

Scenario Two. A reading of signs, *circa* 1980, with less visibility than those painted by the back-to-basics movement of the 1970s, leads one to predict a voucher system. The initiation of a citizens' proposition and its subsequent approval could occur in some state (perhaps California) with stunning rapidity. The appeal would be wrapped in an attractive package of greater parental choice, greater parental control, elimination of a costly administrative bureaucracy, the free enterprise system — all in the name of better schools. Although I believe the voucher plan, as a total system, is seriously flawed, the personal appeal for many will not easily be overcome.

To discuss this scenario further would simply take me into the arguments I forwarded in Chapter Two. I have reservations about the unexamined virtue of more parental choice in the education of their children. I believe that one bureaucracy would be replaced by another. There are no data from the private school experience to suggest that the large number of institutions needed to implement a broad-scale voucher plan would be an improvement. But I believe that a strange assortment of interests could combine to create a voucher system. And I have given no small amount of thought to the personal challenge of trying to eliminate its shortcomings if we should get it.

Scenario Three. Neither of the preceding scenarios appeals to me. The third and fourth scenarios that follow do. The third is not different from the fourth; rather, it is part of it. I would hope to see both scenarios — or, more accurately, the fourth with the third as a composite part — evolving together. They would take place differently in various parts of the country — that is, different ecological relationships and balances would emerge.

Scenario Three is simply a school reconstructed from its

119

present form, as described in Chapter Five, into what I have sketched briefly in the first part of this chapter and in other writings. It is the common school we have long known reconstructed to eliminate as many barriers to equality as possible and to provide greater humanization of knowledge and access to it, with primary attention given to cultivating the personal growth of each student. Also, it is the common school reconstructed to take account of society's changing ability to educate out of schools as well.

My discussion earlier in this chapter of some propositions underlying such a reconstructed school left out essential complementary relationships with the broader culture. Of critical importance is the use of resources in the larger educational ecology for developing individual talent. One of the most powerful educational forces is the role model. Schools are markedly limited in the kind and range of role models they provide. Even when teachers are poets, musicians, sculptors, or photographers, the role they project is primarily one of "teacher." Even when they teach what they do well, as in various industrial arts or athletics, they spend almost all their time with the development of others; their own creative activities occur away from school. I firmly believe that learning occurs best in a laboratory setting where the teacher also is involved in doing and creating, providing a model of a human being as creater.

But even if schools were to be conducted according to such a plan, it is doubtful that there would be a sufficient variety of role models available, especially in small schools, for development of each student's special interests and talents. Consequently, I consider it imperative for young people to have access to persons whose lives and livelihoods revolve around their talents as writers, athletes, scientists, cinematographers, musicians, and the like. Long-term instruction designed for developing embryonic talent might very well be provided by performer-teachers in the private sector. I would endorse the concept of each student having an allocation of vouchers to secure the out-of-school resources for the in-depth cultivation of one or more special interests.

The rumblings of disagreement to my proposal are predictable. Most of them will come from the teaching profession. Teachers will object to noncertified teachers. But let us recall the context of my recommendation. The school is to be more educational than it is now; the major fields of human inquiry will constitute the subject matter for personal encounters and growth. The school, in collaboration with the home, will take responsibility for identification and encouragement of individual talent. But it is costly for schools to provide all of the resources needed. At best, schools can provide only limited opportunities, thus forcing students to bend their interests to those provided. To protest this proposal with the argument that the human resources in the community are noncertified teachers reinforces for me an earlier point — namely, that we are still a weak, divided, insecure profession.

Finally, let me say that it is the idea of assuring development of a talent in each student at each phase of schooling that is important. There is little new in the idea of using community resources for this purpose, except for the added variable of a limited voucher plan. Some schools and communities already have progressed significantly with the logistics of such a plan. What is required now is its implementation for all students.

Scenario Four. The fourth scenario represents a significant step toward the educative society. Essentially, it is a plan for mobilizing all of the available resources for education and cultural enrichment in a community. Because our communities vary so widely, the plans developed would differ from place to place. The plans of cities (London, Paris, New York, Cairo, Tokyo, Singapore, Rio de Janeiro) in different countries might be more alike than the plans of several cities and towns (Detroit, Englewood, Moss Landing, Tombstone, Decatur) in the U.S. But the purpose in each would be the same: to develop and utilize all those resources required for the maximum development of our young people and the continuing educational and cultural well-being of all.

The criterion of success for each institution or agency would be that it functioned without undue stress or strain and with a sense of symmetry as a healthy organism. What it was asked to do and what it did do would be compatible with what those connected with the institution thought it was supposed to do. Do our schools now operate by such a criterion of success?

The nature of interactions among the persons collectively comprising the educational ecosystem would shift according to the particular kinds of needs and demands placed upon the system. For example, a young couple contemplating parenthood could initiate a sequence of interactions designed to prepare them nutritionally, mentally, and emotionally to assist in the early rearing of a child. With entry of the child into school, certain of the relationships already established with other institutions would be maintained. Later, interactions among home, school, and the world of work would increase, as business and industry assumed their proper role in career education and specific vocational training.

Assuming the kind of school described earlier, urban plans would be designed to develop the educational and training capacity of existing institutions and agencies rather than to create new ones. However, new settings for teaching the lower literacies through technology and for developing individual talents would arise. Rural areas might require the construction of community centers where schools, health facilities, specialized training units, and an array of cultural and service resources would be clustered. These would operate 24 hours per day, 365 days a year.

Such a center in an impoverished section of Tehran comes to mind. A cluster of sprawling buildings housed a K-12 school, with many classes organized around the laboratory concept. Also, there were modest outdoor facilities for recreation; clinics for dental work and treatment of minor injuries and health problems; rooms and personnel for adult counseling, from marital to financial; and shops and laboratories essential to hands-on educating. There were two principals, one who spent most of her time in the community and the other who spent most of her time with the internal operation.

I was on the site early in June. Not many people were about; most of these were packing up and cleaning. This was, after all, a school, and the summer recess of three months had arrived. How tragic! Presumably, the educational, health, counseling, and various support needs of the community were now to lie dormant for three months. Good as this facility is in many ways, it provides a striking example as to how each ecosystem comprising the educational and cultural ecology of this community operates according to principles and rules of the dominant institution. In the setting described, school rules dominated all functions, whether or not they were a part of the traditional school functions.

For an educational ecology, to say nothing of a larger ecology embracing training and cultural life, to function well, the decision-making and administrative structures must encompass more than the interests of schooling. Authority and responsibility should be invested in a council or board of trustees representing a cross section of community life. The commissioner or top administrator would be charged with responsibility for the educational commitment of all agencies participating. His or her executive staff (administrative council) would consist of the top educational official of each agency. One of these would be the superintendent of schools.

There is, of course, a fifth scenario. This would be a *school* responsible for everything educational, 24 hours each day, 365 days each year. It would be an expansion of the school we have. Given the tendency of schools to expand upward, downward, and sideways, and the readiness of many people to equate this expansion with universal education and all that is good, such could occur. But I fear that the principles now governing so much of schooling and the criteria commonly used for judging school success would prevail. We would have a much-schooled society but not necessarily an educative one.

⅄ A Final Statement

Central to all that has preceded is my belief in the common school. I regard it not simply as desirable for but as essential to the preservation and cultivation of our democratic way of life and our political democracy. The fact that as individuals and as a nation we have not lived up to our ideals in no way diminishes either the attractiveness of these ideals or their continuing appeal in guiding our actions. Indeed, the obvious gap between the two should challenge the best in us all. The fact that our schools have too often reflected our shortcomings rather than our ideals is no justification for expecting little of them or doing away with them. It is, I think, no accident that this democracy still survives in spite of our errors of commission and omission, and that we have one of the most comprehensive, accessible systems of schooling in the world.

The prime role of our schools is the development of the full potential of each individual. Part of this development is an awareness of the shortcomings between our ideals and our actions and a commitment to mobilize personal resources to do everything possible to rectify these shortcomings. Unfortunately, this process seems to have fallen short. We still face the issue of providing access to opportunities for many people who either do not fully appreciate the role of the common school or who think it has done its job and is no longer necessary. To give up on the common school now would place in doubt the possibility of achieving for all of our people what only some have enjoyed.

Toward the Educative Society

There is little doubt in my mind that the common school is in substantial trouble. Much of this trouble stems from a glaring omission: There has been little dialogue about what our schools are for, what they are asked to do, or what they should do. And we know precious little about what they actually do. One of the surest signs of an institution being in trouble is when there is little informed discussion about it. In few areas of public concern have we allowed opinion to substitute for hard knowledge so consistently.

The trouble stems from errors of commission, too. In a period of simplifying the problems of and trivializing expectations for our schools, external forces (often aided and abetted by educational leaders) have imposed requirements that have exacerbated the already seriously impaired educational function of schools.

The rest of the trouble lies within. Too many of the resources available to the system of schooling go to the maintenance of the system, not to the schools and classrooms where education is to take place. The key role of the principal is ill-defined; an insufficient portion of his or her time is devoted to the instructional program. In general, we have settled for a training-level preparation for teachers rather than for the necessary breadth and depth of general and professional education.

I have provided no panaceas for any of these problems; there is none. I have proposed that we talk about what our common school tradition is and what today's schools are for; about what the educating society does or could do and what would be most critical for schools to do; about what education is and is not; about the kinds of human beings education should help develop; and about what knowledge and processes would be most useful for the personal experiences of becoming. The time taken to write this book will have been well spent if some of the ideas in it help promote the essential dialogue.

I have suggested that the common school, as it exists in each community, is the tangible, natural, manageable place for all of us to come together in making that school more educational and, therefore, more common. I have endeavored to identify some of the shortcomings, opportunities, and challenges of those individuals whose interests and activities impinge on the school. In this, I have attempted to be catholic, whether in criticizing or in suggesting a course of action. We are all accountable for the condition of our schools. This is no time for us to become either defensive or critical of the shortcomings of others. It is the time for all of us to join in reconstructing the common school.

124

References

Chapter One

1. These sources include John I. Goodlad, M. Frances Klein, and Associates, *Looking Behind the Classroom Door* (Worthington, Oh: Charles A. Jones, 1974); John I. Goodlad, M. Frances Klein, Jerrold M. Novotney, and Associates, *Early Schooling in the United States* (New York: McGraw-Hill, 1973); and, when specifically noted, preliminary data from *A Study of Schooling in the United States*, an in-depth study of 38 schools conducted under the auspices of the Institute for Development of Educational Activities, Inc., and supported by a consortium of philanthropic foundations, the National Institute of Education, and the U.S. Office of Education (in progress at the time this manuscript goes to press).

2. Lawrence A. Cremin, "Public Education and the Education of the Public," *Teachers College Record*, September 1975, p. 11.

Chapter Two

1. Robert M. Hutchins, "The Great Anti-School Campaign," *The Great Ideas Today* (Chicago: Encyclopedia Britannica, 1972), p. 154.

2. Peter Shrag, "End of the Impossible Dream," *Saturday Review*, September 1970, p. 68.

3. For further description, see John I. Goodlad, "What Goes On in Our Schools," *Educational Researcher*, March 1977, pp. 3-6; and Harold Shane's interview with John Goodlad, "A Preview of 'Schooling in America,'" *Phi Delta Kappan*, September 1978, pp. 47-50.

4. See reference 1, Chapter One *(Early Schooling in the United States)*.

5. Data from John I. Goodlad and Associates, *A Study of Schooling* (in process). For further information, see reference 3 above.

6. National Council on Educational Research, *Reflections and Recommendations*, Fourth Annual Report (Washington: National Institute of Education; Department of Health, Education, and Welfare, 1978), p. 66.

Chapter Three

1. Lawrence A. Cremin, "Further Notes Toward a Theory of Education," *Notes on Education*, Vol. 4, 1974, p. 1.

2. David S. Saxon, "Is It Time to Stop Learning?" *Newsweek*, June 28, 1976.

3. John Dewey, *Democracy and Education* (New York: Macmillan, 1916), p. 120.

4. Lawrence A. Cremin, *The Transformation of the School* (New York: Alfred A. Knopf, 1961), pp. 122, 123.

5. R.S. Peters, *Ethics and Education* (London: George Allen and Unwin Ltd., 1966), p. 27.

6. John Dewey, op. cit., p. 53.

7. A.N. Whitehead, *The Aims of Education and Other Essays* (New York: Macmillan, 1929), p. 21.

8. Ibid., p. 1.

9. Ibid., pp. 19, 20.

10. Ibid., p. 31.

11. Norman Cousins, "How to Make People Smaller Than They Are," *Saturday Review*, December 1978, p. 15.

12. Robert Rosen, "Do We Really Need Ends to Justify the Means?" *Center Report*, February 1976, pp. 29, 30.

13. Franklin Bobbitt, *How to Make a Curriculum* (Boston: Houghton Mifflin, 1924).

14. Ralph W. Tyler, *Basic Principles of Curriculum and Instruction* (Chicago: University of Chicago Press, 1949).

15. Ibid., p. 58.

16. Ibid., p. 57.

17. Somewhat to its dismay, a Task Force of the National Institute of Education that interviewed individuals from over 60 organizations with presumed interest in curriculum matters found the overriding interest to be having a piece of the action: "While individuals and groups often have strong views on what should and should not be emphasized in school programs, concern for 'who should make curricular decisions?' appears to take priority over the question, 'what shall be taught?' " See National Institute of Education, *Current Issues, Problems, and Concerns in Curriculum Development* (Washington: Department of Health, Education, and Welfare, 1976), p. 3.

18. Joseph J. Schwab, "What Drives the Schools?" Paper prepared for the National Institute of Education (November 3, 1976), mimeographed.

19. I am grateful to Bette Overman, researcher in *A Study of Schooling* (in progress), for her analysis of the data on students', teachers', and parents'. perceptions of school goals.

20. Those primarily involved were Gad Alexander, Betty Bamberg, Jason Frand, M. Frances Klein, Neil Schmidt, and Kenneth A. Tye. I am indebted to them for their work in compiling the list of goals for schooling appearing on these pages.

21. A.N. Whitehead, op. cit., p. 22.

22. Norman Cousins, op. cit., p. 15.

23. Data on physical education analyzed by Kenneth A. Tye; data on the arts analyzed by Joyce Wright (both researchers in *A Study of Schooling*).

24. John Dewey, op. cit., p. 192.

25. These data are from *A Study of Schooling*, analyzed by Joyce Wright.

26. Clifford F.S. Bebell, "The Educational Program: Part One," in *Emerging Designs for Education: Program, Organization, Operation and Finance* (Denver, Colo.: Designing Education for the Future, an Eight-State Project, 1968), pp. 51-54.

27. Gunnar Myrdal was very perceptive in noting that American society is not and has not been without a comparatively clear and well-articulated sense of goals. We appear to have been more sure about them than have most nations

about theirs. However, the ideals stated in them, Myrdal points out, are sufficiently lofty to sharpen awareness of our failure to live up to them, arousing in successive generations a sense of sin. See Gunnar Myrdal, with the assistance of Richard Sterne and Arnold Rose, *An American Dilemma: The Negro Problem and Modern Democracy* (New York: Harper and Row, 1944).

Chapter Four

1. Robert Rosen, "Do We Really Need Ends to Justify the Means?" *Center Report,* February 1976, pp. 29, 30.
2. Stephen K. Bailey, *The Purposes of Education* (Bloomington, Ind.: Phi Delta Kappa, 1976), pp. 61, 76.
3. Hope Jensen Leichter, *The Family as Educator* (New York: Teachers College Press, Columbia University, 1975).
4. For further analysis of the model as employed for school improvement, see Ernest R. House, *The Politics of Educational Innovation* (Berkeley: Calif.: McCutchan, 1974)
5. Seymour B. Sarason, *The Culture of the School and the Problem of Change* (Boston: Allyn and Bacon, 1971).
6. John I. Goodlad, *Facing the Future* (New York: McGraw-Hill, 1976), p. 151.
7. Elliot W. Eisner, "On the Uses of Educational Connoisseurship and Criticism for Evaluating Classroom Life," *Teachers College Record,* February 1977, p. 351.
8. William James, *Pragmatism* (New York: Longmans, Green, 1909).
9. Ramón Margolef, *Perspectives in Ecological Theory* (Chicago: University of Chicago Press, 1968), p. 4.

Chapter Five

1. See the bibliography on educational change prepared by Lillian K. Drag, in John I. Goodlad, *The Dynamics of Educational Change: Toward Responsive Schools* (New York: McGraw-Hill, 1975), pp. 224-49.
2. For further elaboration, see Seymour B. Sarason, *Human Services and Resource Networks: Rationale, Possibilities, and Public Policies* (San Francisco: Jossey-Bass, 1977).
3. Thomas Sowell, "Patterns of Black Excellence," *The Public Interest,* Spring 1976, pp. 26-58.
4. Garlie A. Forehand and Marjorie Ragosta, *A Handbook for Integrated Schooling* (Washington: U.S. Department of Health, Education, and Welfare, 1976).
5. Harvey A. Averch *et al, How Effective Is Schooling?* (Englewood Cliffs, N.J.: Educational Technology Publications, 1974), p. 171.
6. For reviews of research on teaching in which the authors have extrapolated as to make their interpretations of research useful for teachers, see Michael J. Dunkin and Bruce J. Biddle, *The Study of Teaching* (New York: Holt, Rinehart and Winston, 1974); and Jacob S. Kounin, *Discipline and Group Management in Classrooms* (New York: Holt, Rinehart and Winston, 1970).
7. Benjamin S. Bloom, *Human Characteristics and School Learning* (New York: McGraw-Hill, 1976).
8. A model of major factors that has proved useful for research and also is useful for instruction is that of John B. Carroll, "A Model of School Learning," *Teachers College Record,* May 1963, pp. 723-33.

9.   I have attempted to deal with some of these elsewhere. See, in particular, John I. Goodlad, "The Reconstruction of Teacher Education," *Teachers College Record,* September 1970, pp. 61-71.

10.   Saul Bellow, "The Challenge," address delivered at the Nobel Foundation, Stockholm, 1976.

11.   Gary D. Fenstermacher, unpublished remarks to Board of Education, San Diego Unified School District, February 10, 1977.

12.   See Jacob W. Getzels and Egon G. Guba, "Social Behavior and the Administrative Process," *School Review,* Winter, 1957.

13.   Raymond E. Callahan, *Education and the Cult of Efficiency* (Chicago: University of Chicago Press, 1962).

14.   Bellow, op. cit.

15.   Goodlad, *The Dynamics of Educational Change,* op. cit.

Chapter Six

1.   Charles W. Rusch, "MOBOC: A Mobile Learning Environment," in Gary J. Coates (ed.), *Alternative Learning Environments* (Strasburg, Pa.: Dowden, Hutchinson and Ross, 1974).

2.   Data from *A Study of Schooling* on teachers' resources for teaching, compiled and analyzed by researcher M. Frances Klein.

3.   Joseph W. Gauld, "A Better Way for American Education" (mimeo), p. 7. Paper provided through personal correspondence.

4.   Ibid.

5.   Marshall Gordon, "Conflict and Liberation: Personal Aspects of the Mathematics Experience," *Curriculum Inquiry,* Fall 1978, p. 252.

6.   Data from *A Study of Schooling* on tracking, compiled and analyzed by researcher Jeannie Oakes.

7.   Wellford Wilms, *Public and Proprietary Vocational Training: A Study of Effectiveness* (Lexington, Mass.: D.C. Heath Lexington Books, 1975).

8.   John I. Goodlad, *Facing the Future: Issues in Education and Schooling* (New York: McGraw-Hill, 1976), chap. 16.

9.   Data from A Study of Schooling on physical education, compiled and analyzed by researcher Kenneth A. Tye.